THE *THINKING CLEARLY* SERIES
Series editor: Clive Calver

The *Thinking Clearly* series sets out the main issues in a variety of important subjects. Written from a mainstream Christian standpoint, the series combines clear biblical teaching with up-to-date scholarship. Each of the contributors is an authority in his or her field. The series is written in straightforward everyday language, and each volume includes a range of practical applications and guidance for further reading.

The series has two main aims:
1. To help Christians understand their faith better
2. To show how Christian truths can illuminate matters of crucial importance in our society.

D1189148

THE THINKING CLEARLY SERIES
Series Editor: Clive Calver

Thinking Clearly About God and Science

ROB FROST
&
DAVID WILKINSON

MONARCH

EVANGELICAL ALLIANCE
STRUIK CHRISTIAN BOOKS

British Library Cataloguing Data
A Catalogue record for this book is available
from the British Library

ISBN 1 85424 333 0

Co-published with:

The Evangelical Alliance,
Whitefield House, 186 Kennington Park Road,
London SE11 4BT.

Struik Christian Books Ltd.,
Cornelis Struik House, 80 McKenzie Street,
Cape Town 8001, South Africa.
Reg no 04/02203/06

Designed and produced by
Bookprint Creative Services
P.O. Box 827, BN21 3YJ, England for
MONARCH PUBLICATIONS
Broadway House, The Broadway,
Crowborough, East Sussex, TN6 1HQ.
Printed in Great Britain

Contents

Foreword

By Sir John Houghton, CBE, FRS

*Co-chairman of the Science Assessment Working Group
of the Intergovernmental panel on Climate Change and
former Chief Executive of the Meteorological Office*

During the second half of the twentieth century we have seen, in the Western world, a general retreat from religion. It has seemed increasingly irrelevant to our materialist culture. Even some theologians have joined this retreat in going so far as to say that God is dead!

There has also been a growing disillusionment with science. Science and technology continually demonstrate to us their power and potential to increase our happiness and our quality of life. Yet, in practice they seem constantly to fail to deliver. Hence the disillusionment – which arises largely from a misunderstanding of what science is about and what it can and cannot do.

Because religion (especially traditional religion) is no longer seen as important and science cannot produce the real answers, life for many seems empty and futile. The young especially are desperately asking basic questions – where can I find meaning, what is life all about, where can I find answers?

This book has been written to help to counter this slide into meaninglessness. Very emphatically it argues that God is far from dead; in fact he is very much alive. Science too is relevant not just for what it can do and the good things it can provide,

7

but because scientific thinking itself can also help in this quest for meaning. Because God is Creator and intimately concerned with his creation and because science is the study of that creation, science too can help in the search for God.

But the book has not just been written to present an argued case for God or for science. It is also a book about people; the disciplines of theology and science cannot be divorced from the people who pursue them or who are affected by them. First and foremost it is about the authors, one a scientist and one an evangelist who explain why they believe and expose some of their own pathways to belief. They also quote extensively from distinguished scientists who have found belief in God to be both meaningful and relevant.

Above all they constantly present to us to the person of Jesus who brings together in a unique way the disciplines of theology (because Jesus is God) and science (because Jesus is the agent of creation). When you have read the book, I am sure that the authors' desire is that you find, not only that you have in some sense met them, but that you have also met their Lord whom they present so eloquently.

John Houghton

Preface

This book is the result of a collaboration between someone trained as a scientist and someone whose science training ended at school! Nevertheless we both share an excitement in science and the conviction that the Lordship of Christ means that the Christian faith should be relevant to all aspects of life. We have tried to maintain the slightly different perspectives between us by writing separate chapters, although that should not be taken as an indication that we have differing views.

Neither of us are primarily academics. We write out of a love and commitment of sharing the good news of Jesus.

For the Christian believer, we hope that this book will be a help in living out the Christian faith in a scientific culture. We need to do some work if we are going to be effective missionaries in our culture which has to such a large part been shaped by science. Too often the church has left scientists who are Christians stranded on a desert island without the support and theological resources which could undergird their day to day work and witness.

For those who read this book who are not Christians, may we suggest that you might find that some of the 'scientific' walls that seemed such a barrier against Christian faith, may in fact be less solid than you thought.

This is a book that was not worked out in the study but very much in the dialogue with many others throughout the world. For the many questions, comments, conversations and ideas we are thankful. In particular, we need to thank a number of people:

- Tony Collins, Alison Wilkinson and Clive Calver for their encouragement and comments on the manuscript.
- Everyone who discussed this project with Rob during the hectic summer of 1995 with apologies if he bored you with the subject.
- Derek and Pauline Harrison for late night mind reeling discussions at Underscar Manor Hotel.
- Alan and Jill, practising scientists, who travelled on pilgrimage through Israel and helped earth some of the issues.
- Rob's son Andy, and his teenage friends Jason, Pete, Joanna, Nal, Chris, Jem, Sarah, Graham, Olly, Jez, and Luke who reminded Rob of the purpose of this book during a crazy week of sun and surf in Perranporth.
- Elm Hall Drive Methodist Church and Liverpool Methsoc who again generously allowed David the time to do this project.
- Leo Osborn, Nick Redman, Ajay George, Dr Rob Gayton, Vivien Redman, Janet Kermode, Alison Rollins, and Karen Sutton for their support.
- Andy Hall for his help with the references.
- Alison and Adam who have been a constant source of encouragement and help to David, sacrificially giving their time and love.

Rob Frost
David Wilkinson
September 1995.

About the Authors

Rob Frost's failure to pass GCSE science equips him to make science subjects approachable to a non-scientific audience! He has a passion for Christian apologetics, and has led seminars on science and faith at three Spring Harvests and at a number of Universities around the country. He is the co-ordinator of 'Easter People', a holiday convention for 7000 Christians; director of 'Seed Teams', year-long frontline mission programmes in the UK and overseas; and he leads over fifty missions with a team exceeding 500 each year. He was awarded a doctorate by London University in 1995 for his thesis on contemporary missiology. He is married to Jacqui, and has two teenage sons.

His books include *Big Questions, Conversation Starters, Go for Growth, People at Work, Visions, Break Me, Shape Me, Breaking Bread, Pilgrims, Gospel End, Broken Cross, Burning Questions, When I Can't Pray*.

David Wilkinson is married to Alison with a son Adam. He has a PhD in Theoretical Astrophysics and is a Fellow of the Royal Astronomical Society. He did research on a wide range of topics from cosmology to the death of the dinosaurs! He is a minister at Elm Hall Drive Methodist Church in Liverpool, and Chaplain at Liverpool University. He speaks and broadcasts widely on the relationship of science and religion.

His books include *In the Beginning God* and *God, the Big Bang and Stephen Hawking*.

1

Myths Or Reality?

(Rob Frost & David Wilkinson)

In this opening chapter we introduce the thinking behind the structure of the book, in particular that we need to explode some powerful myths that are believed about the relationship of science and Christianity.

'World War II bomber found on the moon!' is one of the more famous tabloid newspaper headlines along with 'Freddie Starr ate my hamster'! Neither is true but there will be people around Great Britain who will repeat these headlines to their friends, justifying them with 'but it said it in the papers' or 'my friend told me so'. They are entertaining stories, but are so ludicrous that most of us can dismiss them.

Yet there are other statements that are more difficult to dismiss. In fact you need to know quite a bit to see whether they are true or false. Does water, when going down a plug hole, rotate in different directions depending on whether you are in the Northern hemisphere or the Southern hemisphere? You may have heard of such a thing, or even seen entertainers on the equator do such a demonstration. Is it true or is it just an entertainer's trick? To know the answer to that question you actually need to know quite a bit about science.

Some of these 'myths' can control attitude and behaviour. This is often the case in the 'slimming' culture. For example some believe that eating grapefruit can burn off fat as it contains special enzymes which dissolve body fat. It sounds quite scientific and a great idea! As long as you have grapefruit as a starter, you can eat as much steak, chips and chocolate cake as you like! Of course, it is unfortunately quite untrue.

This book is written to combat some very powerful myths. They are not myths about slimming or hamsters but about the relationship of science and religion. Some are quite silly and yet are believed widely. Some are half truths which give a misleading picture. Some can only be seen as false if you get to know quite a bit of the background in terms of science, history and religious thought. Many do control attitude and behaviour, on the one hand building a barrier for many to Christian faith, while on the other keeping those with Christian faith well away from experiencing the excitement of science.

They are the type of statements that you can hear in the local pub and the local University. Russell Stannard, former Professor of Physics at the Open University, once collected thirty of these myths that were used as 'scientific arguments against religion'. They were things such as:

- the persecution of Galileo was typical of the Church's attitude to scientific progress
- most scientists are atheists
- Freud says religious believers are simply neurotic.

In *Behold the Front Page!* a very clever lampoon of how tabloid journalists would rewrite the Bible, the 'ten things you need to know about God' includes such things as 'no one knows why he invented wasps' and 'he has a flair for creativity – look at giraffes'! It also lists God's dislikes as 'Charles Darwin, Albert Einstein and the Bishop of Durham'![1] Even in his recent book, *River out of Eden*[2], the Oxford biologist and popular author, Richard Dawkins, while raging against the suggestion that the Universe was created actually falls into the trap of many such caricatures of religion.

These myths of the supposed conflict of science and religion are rarely justified, but trotted out on the basis of 'scientists tell us' or 'everyone knows that'. They actually arise from an inadequate understanding of history, science and theology. The trouble is that not only are they used to attack Christian faith, they are often believed by Christians themselves. Christians have often been 'squeezed into the world's mould', to use J B Phillips' translation of Romans 12:2, accepting these half truths. The result is that within many churches 'science' is seen as an enemy. Scientists in the congregation are viewed with fear and suspicion, and scientific discoveries are greeted with scepticism and confusion.

We therefore need to think clearly about science, and this is what we attempt to do in this book. We have selected six of these myths, as a way of getting deeper into science and theology. Through this method we will be able to address questions such as what should be the Christian attitude to science, what is the Creator God like and how can he be known, and how does God work in the Universe.

We are conscious that we are not giving a comprehensive account of all the aspects of the relationship between science and religion. Indeed, there is not just one easy way of thinking about this relationship. However, we hope in the six areas to explode some commonly held myths, to excite you with science and the Bible and to establish some principles which will provide a framework for those who want to think further and in different areas of science.

The myths themselves sound simple, and in a sense that is their power. The reality is much more complex, and because of that at times is frustrating. To expose the reality behind the myths actually needs some hard work, and the results are sometimes surprising.

Yet we write out of the conviction that all truth is God's truth. If there are unanswered questions, difficult concepts and hard work along the way, then that is part of our pilgrim journey as Christians. This is not a book that claims to give ready made and easy answers, but we hope that through it tools can be gained to live in an increasingly complex world.

Professor H H Huxley recently told of an incident where he was asked by a hitchhiker for a lift in his car. The hitchhiker was somewhat optimistic as he was wearing a T-shirt with the slogan 'Rage against the Machine'! We need to be searching for integrity in what we believe and how we live.

2

Can God Be Proved By Science?
(Rob Frost)

If God could be proved, there would be no need for faith. Whilst science can neither prove nor disprove God, it often raises important questions about meaning, purpose and life which we need to face up to. These questions provide an important context for discussing the existence of God, and they are questions which may lead us to discover true faith in God.

What happened?

Last year my home was burgled. Quite a lot of things were taken including a video recorder, stereo-cassette and some jewellery which meant a great deal to my wife. The police came and made sympathetic noises. When they realised that the burglar had left a complete set of fingerprints on the window where he gained entry, however, they became much more interested. At least, they had some evidence!

Three days later, the same burglar broke into another house nearby. As he was escaping, he got trapped in the small entrance way between the main house and the porch door. To his acute embarrassment, his 'loot' was trapped with him! Some workmen heard his exasperated cries and called the police. When the police patrol arrived, they found the burglar in a somewhat desperate state, and uttering the familiar words 'it's a fair cop!' This time, they had not only got evidence, they had got proof!

I am very suspicious of anyone, be they scientist, theologian, philosopher or evangelist who claims to be able to 'prove God'. They'd have to trap the Lord of all Creation in a box and display him to the general public for all to see! All sense of faith, mystery and infinity would be gone for ever and he'd be about as special as a god made of stone, wood or steel.

We can't prove God by science, or by any other means. But we can produce evidence which points to the existence of God and to God's creative purposes, and it's evidence which demands a verdict!

When the police arrived at my home to examine the evidence and to survey the crime scene, they worked their way through a basic list of questions which they'd used in countless previous situations. Questions which are the backbone of every enquiry whether it's in criminology, journalism or science.

First there was the 'what happened?' line of questioning. As they examined the broken window, the disturbed drawers and the strewn clothing they seemed only to be interested in the story of what had taken place.

This kind of question is at the heart of any discussion on the existence of God. 'What happened' to make the Universe come into being, what was the first cause of the cosmos? This is a question which can lead us, very quickly, into complicated philosophical and theological arguments!

When the scientist begins to ask 'what happened', or 'what was the cause of the Universe?' he's asking philosophical questions which have exercised generations of the world's greatest thinkers.

Starting with Plato

Plato (427–347BC) pointed out in his 'Laws' that things in the Universe move or change. Motion or change in one thing is caused by motion or change in something else which affects it. This great philosopher went on to suggest that the presence of motion or change in the Universe is only explicable if, eventually, you go back far enough to reach the origin of this apparently endless series of causes. He concluded that motion or change must originate in an initial self-moved mover or 'soul'. Plato concluded that this soul is 'the source of change and motion' in 'all that is, or has become, or will be.'

If we accept the idea that something real cannot be produced out of nothing, then there must, it is argued, be a first, necessary, uncaused being which is the source of being in everything else.

Take this idea a stage further, and we discover that the 'first mover' must have all of the qualities found in the Universe because there can be nothing in a creature which is not first in its creator. Because this being is absolutely primary, it will have all of the qualities of the Universe in a perfect form.

Thomas Aquinas (1225–1274) was one of the first to popularise the concept of cause and effect in relation to the Universe. He argued that we all live in a world of cause and effect. Every effect can be explained in terms of a cause. That cause in turn can be explained by what causes lie behind it. He went on to say that everything that is, came from something else.

I came from my parents, they from theirs, and so on right back through to the first signs of life on the planet. Earth itself came from the Sun. The Sun is a star among many stars. Stars were formed by collapsing clouds of hydrogen gas, but then what caused the hydrogen atoms?

This concept of cause and effect holds for whatever particular theory of creation history you may hold. Who made Adam and Eve? Where did the cosmic dust come from? Who was responsible for what the scientists call the Big Bang, the origin of the Universe itself? What caused matter in the first place?

These ideas were expanded by René Descartes (1596-1650) who is often labelled 'the father of modern philosophy'. Descartes advocated that the first cause must be separate, independent and self determining or it is merely another step in the process. He argued that our very existence leads us to the idea of a perfect being: God.

A reason for something?

Leibniz, in his *Theodicy* (written in 1710) said that 'the great principle' of this 'cause and effect' argument was that 'nothing takes place without a sufficient reason'. He found this philosophically satisfying. If this is not the case, we are looking at a very different kind of universe. If we imagine that the world has been everlasting and that it has been going on and on in time forever, then we may travel back in time for ever but never reach a sufficient explanation of its existence.

He suggested that such an infinite process of 'cause and effect' pointed only to a world of total meaninglessness, something which he found intellectually unsatisfactory. He concluded, therefore, that the whole Universe depends on God, who is uncaused and does not depend on anything else. If God was not the first mover, the only alternative is a cosmos which has been self-perpetuating eternally. Does it take more faith to hold to such a theory than to accept some divine origin, or 'first mover' to all things? What is the alternative to God?

We shall see in Chapter Five that modern theories about the origin of the Universe make some of these questions more complicated, but the question why is there something rather than nothing, still may be a pointer to God.

Not what but why?

The day after my house was burgled the detective arrived. When he examined the crime scene he probed more deeply than the uniformed officers, and his line of questioning seemed more purposeful and detailed. He was not only interested in what had happened, but why? Why did the burglar choose this point of entry? Why did he take some items but leave others? And why did he choose our house and not the others in the street?

The question 'why?' should also be applied to the cosmos. Yet it's a question which many of us in contemporary secularised society would rather not ask. We're not particularly interested in the reason 'why'!

We are cocooned in neon filled cities, away from the starlit sky or the ocean's mighty surf. We mark the turning of the years with digital accuracy without pausing to enjoy the intricate changes of the passing seasons. We fill up our time asking 'what's next?' without stopping to ask the question 'why?'

The question 'why?' is disturbing and powerful. It leads us to choose a universe devoid of meaning or one filled with divine purpose. It makes us face up to the most fundamental question of all – 'Is there some meaning to our existence?'

Scientists involved in research which takes them to the limit of human knowledge are personally exposed to these fundamental questions of meaning. When the scientist asks the question 'why', he will quickly cross from science into the disciplines of philosophy and theology.

A common characteristic of scientists is the ability to ask the question 'why?', so it's little wonder that many scientists are interested in issues such as the 'first cause'. Their discipline teaches them to look for answers and to use imagination in the interpretation of results.

A couple of years ago Channel 4 television hosted a fascinating debate about the existence of God as part of a series of discussions from Oxford University. One of the leading speakers was the philosopher, Professor Richard Swinburne, who opened the batting for the 'pro-existence' team by pinpointing the limitations of science. 'Science cannot explain why the basic laws of nature are as they are,' he said, 'this is where science starts from, what it explains other things in terms of.'

When we move into a discussion of 'why' things are the way they are, one would expect scientists to withdraw from the debate and to let philosophers and theologians take the stand. Recently, however, more and more scientists are moving into these other areas, and opening up questions of meaning traditionally posed by other disciplines.

Why are so many scientists asking why?

Perhaps the most outstanding example is the astrophysicist Stephen Hawking. He has made a significant contribution to the debate about the origins of the universe, and his personal quest for a 'theory of everything' is well known by many people who are not scientists. Hawking, a Fellow of the Royal Society at thirty-two, Lucasian Professor of Mathematics at Cambridge at thirty-seven, and Commander of the British Empire, has suggested that the Universe has no cause in space or time. Yet one of the motivating forces behind his research is his desire to discover a 'theory of everything', a theory which might help us to solve these 'why?' questions once and for all. He wrote:

'If we do discover a complete theory, it should in time be understandable in broad principle by everyone, not just a few scientists. Then we shall all, philosophers, scientists, and just ordinary people, be able to take part in the discussion of the question of why it is that we and the Universe exist. If we find the answer to that, it would be the ultimate triumph of human reason – for then we would know the mind of God.'[3]

Over many centuries lots of famous philosophers have struggled with the question 'why?'. Why does the Universe exist? Why is it the way that it is? Why does it seem to express some purpose within its being? It is these questions which are being picked up today by scientists.

Jonathan Swift wrote the famous and much-quoted illustration: 'That the Universe was formed by a fortuitous concourse of atoms, I will no more believe than that the accidental jumbling of the alphabet would fall into a most ingenious treatise of philosophy.'

In popular jargon this argument has often been quoted 'if you threw all the letters of the alphabet in the air, would they produce a Shakespearean play?' If such a simple feat is not possible, the argument continues, how could the Universe have developed by sheer chance?

Swift's personal conviction was that the Universe holds a deep purpose. It is such a conviction which, perhaps surprisingly, has become much more popular again in contemporary scientific discussion. Perhaps scientists sense a uniqueness about the Universe that makes it seem unlikely that it originated by sheer 'chance'.

Many contemporary philosophers have also been active in the 'why' questioning which looks at ultimate meanings. On 7th April 1980, *Time* Magazine reported that:

> 'In a quiet revolution in thought and argument that no-one could have foreseen only two decades ago, God is making a comeback. Now it is more respectable among philosophers than it has been for a generation to talk about the possibility of God's existence.'

As philosophers have struggled with the 'why' question from their perspective, contemporary scientists have been writing a great deal from their viewpoint. Roger Penrose is currently Rouse Ball Professor of Mathematics at the Mathematical Institute in Oxford, and his work on stars and black holes is well known. He said on the Channel 4 programme:

> 'There is a certain sense in which I would say that the Universe has a purpose. It's not just there by chance. Some people take the view that the Universe is simply there and it runs along – it's a bit as though it just sort of computes, and we happen by accident to find ourselves in this thing. I don't think that's a very fruitful or helpful way of looking at the Universe.'

Several months after my fateful burglary I got a very official letter from the police station. It stated that the burglar had admitted his offence, and that the mystery of my burglary was now 'cleared up'. I never saw my video recorder, stereo cassette or my wife's jewellery again, but it was some consolation to know that the mystery intruder was a mystery no more.

The 'what' and 'why' questions will never completely 'clear

up' the mystery of the existence of God, reveal God's true identity, or provide cast-iron proof of his existence. They are, however, a very useful starting point for anyone who wants to explore the possibility of God's existence.

Paul Davies, Professor of Mathematical Physics at Adelaide University, is a well-known advocate of this kind of thinking. He does not argue from a committed Christian or religious standpoint, but he was awarded the prestigious Templeton Prize in 1995 for 'progress in religion'. The following day he wrote:

'I am therefore impressed by the extraordinary ingenuity, felicity, and harmony of the laws of physics. It is hard to accept that something so elegantly clever exists without a deeper reason or purpose . . . I have no idea what the Universe is about, but that it is about something I have no doubt.'[4]

John Polkinghorne, President of Queens' College, Cambridge, a Professor of Mathematical Physics who became an Anglican minister seventeen years ago, commented:

'What is interesting about Davies is that he is not attached to any religious tradition. He looks in wonder at the order of the Universe, the science of mind if you like, the fruitfulness of cosmic history and says. 'There is more to be told here; there is some sort of intelligence or purpose for intelligence in cosmic history.' I agree. I think you can learn something about God that way.'[5]

As we look back through the millennia to ask 'what' started all things, our minds may reel at the enormity of the question! As we look at the uniqueness of the Universe, and study its minute and perfect detail, we are confronted with the question 'why?' Such questions may lead us to face the purpose of our existence. These are questions which many scientists are beginning to ask, and questions which, in the scientific context can be difficult to avoid.

The 'what' and 'why' questions may lead the police to

apprehend an illegal intruder but they will never reveal the mysteries of God. If they help us to discover that behind the 'whats' and the 'whys' of the cosmos there is a prime mover, a first cause, a supreme purpose, and a theory of everything, we have found the starting place for belief in God.

Odds on favourite

The lady on the telephone asked me one simple question. 'Do you believe in gambling?' I laughed. 'Of course not. Why do you ask?' 'Can you fly to Newcastle on the first available plane and take part in a television debate?' I looked at my diary. 'Okay!' She breathed a sigh of relief.

It was a fascinating experience. It was Derby day in Epsom, and the programme had contributions from the racecourse as well as from a panel and audience in the studio. The fruit machine manufacturer, the game-show host, the addicted gambler, the 'punters' at Epsom and myself as the 'puritan type' set to work on the subject – with TV presenter Anne Diamond doing her best to keep some kind of order.

The subject turned to 'odds', and I was relieved that on the way up to Newcastle I'd researched some figures to throw into the debate! Even as I quoted them, they seemed unimaginable; and some of the enthusiastic gamblers in the studio audience seemed genuinely surprised by what I'd uncovered!

Roulette turns out to be one of the most likely ways of winning at gambling – but be sure you bet your pound on one number and leave it there while the wheel spins twice. If your number comes up both times you've won £1,296, and the odds of this happening are 1,368 to one against.

In order to win a million pounds for a one pound stake at the races you would probably pick out five horses and bet on them in an accumulator. The odds against achieving it are around two million to one against.

Of course, the worst odds of all are those in the National Lottery. Even small Lottery prizes are not a good gamble. In order to win £1,500 the odds against picking the right five numbers are about 55,000:1. To get an even money chance of winning the jackpot, you'd have to spend £5 a week on tickets for the next 28,000 years! Even then, you might still have to share the prize money!

These odds, however, are far better than the mathematical probability of DNA, the basic structure of life, forming of its own accord. Scientists, whose training and discipline leads them to rely heavily on facts and certainties, do not make good gamblers!

The Lottery of Life?

Richard Dawkins has popularised theories of chance in his book *The Blind Watchmaker*, but still many leading scientists find it completely impossible to accept that the first living cell could have originated by accident. Just to display the possible variations of the genetic code in the DNA molecules making up the chromosomes of one mammalian cell would require about one million pages of eight by eleven inch paper.[6]

An international gathering of mathematicians in Philadelphia in 1969 looked at the probability of the evolution of life developing from an inorganic source. They concluded that the probability of such a complex chain of small inter-connecting molecular units joining together in the formation of DNA was microscopic.

If we take the complex structure of protein as just one example of mathematical probability, we can begin to calculate the 'odds'. To work properly each protein must have exactly the right sequence of amino acid 'beads', and the possibilities are endless! An examination of the protein called pro-insulin, for example, reveals that there are eighty-one amino acid 'beads' in its chain. The chances of a hundred bead chain forming correctly are ten with 129 zeros after it!

Tim Hawthorne, Professor of Biochemistry at the University of Nottingham Medical School computes that the problem of the origin of life comes down to the problem of arranging a 'DNA necklace' of 10,000 beads in the correct order!

'In such a case there would be $10^{8,000}$ possible arrangements ... Then you must stick the nucleotide beads together – a process needing a great deal of chemical energy.'[7]

The number '$10^{8,000}$' is a shorthand way of writing the number ten followed by 8,000 zeros, a number which if written out would cover three and a half pages of this book!

Mark Doughty, an academic from Montreal, reviewing these sort of figures on the probability of life, observed that: 'Nearly all modern physicists find such facts so striking that they are forced to wonder aloud philosophically or even theologically'[8].

It is little wonder, therefore, that Dr Lipson, one of the contributors to the Philadelphia Conference of 1969 said 'Very reluctantly, I now take the view that evolution can't be a chance process, and I now postulate the notion of a Creator.'

The improbability of such an event has therefore led to many strange theories as to how it could have happened. Sir Fred Hoyle, one of the greatest scientists of our generation, felt that the chance of such chains forming by themselves was practically impossible. This conclusion led him to work with Wickramasinghe on a theory that life came here from outer space in the form of a micro-organism.[9]

Francis Crick, who shared a Nobel prize for his work on DNA suggests that some mystical intelligence dispatched life to the earth from the depths of space. One of his explanations as to how it happened was that 'Micro-organisms travelled in the head of an unmanned spaceship sent to earth by a higher civilisation which developed elsewhere some billions of years ago.'[10]

Christians find it much more intellectually satisfying to believe that God was active in the process of creation, in the formation of matter and in the origins of life. The odds of it all happening by itself are not favourable! In fact, you'd stand a lot more chance of winning the National Lottery!

The sensitive balance of the Universe

The Universe of which we are a part exists with a delicate balance of gravity, electromagnetism, and nuclear forces. The delicate symmetry necessary for the existence of this Universe has been likened to an object held in perfect tension by a number of interconnecting springs. The springs are so finely balanced that the slightest change in any one of them would destroy everything: likewise with the Universe.

In reviewing this delicate symmetry, Professor Paul Davies concludes that at the very least, the Universe was an extraordinary accident. He goes on to argue that the only possible explanation for the existence of the Universe was that it was somehow selected out of all possible universes so that human beings could exist. To put it simply, the world was made for man and woman!

Frank J Tipler, who is Professor of Mathematical Physics at Tulane University, Florida, and advocates this explanation which is known as the 'anthropic principle', goes much further. He even suggests that something capable of transcending space-time, with an overview of the entire Universe, may have been involved in the production of a Universe friendly to human beings. If this is the case the Universe was created so that we could be here to observe it. Tipler suggests that theology is a branch of physics and that physicists can infer, by calculation, the existence of God.

If I was a gambling man I would not risk my money on the atheistic gospel of microscopic chance! The mathematical probability of DNA forming and the chance of the delicate symmetry of the Universe being held in just the right tension is so minute as to be completely unacceptable. It makes the odds on winning the National Lottery appear to be positively benevolent.

I do not believe that we are players in a lottery of improbabilities, but part of a cosmos which has a plan, a purpose and a destiny. The odds on favourite is that the Universe came into being not by chance, but on purpose. Not because the 'right environment' for life happened to emerge, but because God willed it to be so! To put it simply, Christians believe that the right environment for human life was created, not by chance, but by Almighty God.

The millions who place their stake on the Lottery every week on the slim chance of winning a fortune seem to do so without ever contemplating the odds. The chance that 'it could be you' seems to blind them from reckoning with the laws of probability.

Those who preach a life without a creator, time without eternity and a world without God would also appear to be gambling against greater odds. Sadly, in the game of life, there is much more to lose than money.

Designer Cosmos

Some Christians might question whether this chapter should be written at all, and suggest that God cannot be argued like some debater's proposition. They would say that he is encountered, and we encounter him in moments of mystery and majesty which can never be fully explained. I have some sympathy for this viewpoint, and have known several experiences of 'encounter' which I could not begin to define. One such moment happened to me when I was on holiday in Tunisia several years ago.

We were awoken at around 3:30 am by our tourist guide. It was already hot. We soon clambered aboard the cool air-conditioned coach and sped away from the oasis and into the darkness of the Sahara Desert.

Eventually we arrived at a place called the Salt Sea, where we obediently climbed out of the coach and followed our guide along a dark path until he told us to line up and be quiet! Nothing could have prepared me for the breathtaking experience which followed. Seconds later the first rays of dawn appeared, and the sky was transformed into brilliant hues of red, yellow and blue.

Gradually the sun peeked over the horizon and the pure white landscape which surrounded us reflected the brilliance of the dawn. He need not have told us to be quiet, for everyone stood in silent awe at the wonder of creation. It was indescribably spectacular!

Most of us at some time in our lives have stopped at a scene of grandeur or beauty and stood silently in amazement. For Christians, experiences like this are evidence that a creative personality has been at work in the beautiful design and order of the cosmos. We believe that God imagined this wonderful world and that he brought it into being.

As I look around the room where I write it is full of my wife's creativity! The pictures on the wall that she drew, the posters of plays that she produced, the sharp black and white decor that she chose, and the beautiful long curtains that she made. I love this study-room because it tells me so much of Jacqui's creativity and artistic flair. The place where I am working is full of evidence of the imagination and design of the one who created it! A stranger could learn a great deal about my wife from studying this room because it's an expression of her personality.

For many, the 'argument of design', or the 'teleological argument' as it's classically known, is a concept which is both helpful and convincing. It reminds us that our world is not just a result of 'happenstance' but something which speaks of creative imagination from every rose petal, rainbow and snowflake.

The philosopher Kant said that 'it always deserves to be mentioned with respect' as 'the oldest, the clearest, and the most accordant with the common reason of mankind.'

I am always personally struck at the intricate order of creation. Commonal garden lupins, for example, have no nectar. The bees which visit them come to collect pollen which they take back to the hive for food. The weight of the bee, when it lands on the flower's beautifully coloured wings, pushes down these two petals and the petals of the keel. The pollen from the anthers has collected in the tip of the keel and as the petals are pressed down, the stigma and long stamens push the pollen out from the keel and on to the underside of the bee.

The bee, with pollen grains sticking to its body, then flies to another flower. If this flower is older than the first one, it may already have lost its pollen. When the bee's weight pushes the keel down, only the stigma comes out and touches the insect's body, picking up the pollen grains on its sticky surface. The process of fertilisation is complete.

The delicacy, order and intricacy of such a process certainly speaks to me of design rather than 'happenstance'!

From design to a Designer?

This argument of design is nothing new, it was first recorded by Xenophon in 390 BC when he quoted Socrates as saying: 'With such signs of forethought in the design of living creatures, can you doubt they are the work of choice or design?' Plato also suggested that observation of the Universe leads us to conclude that there is a designer.

The classic expression of this theory, however, came in William Paley's book *Natural Theology* published in 1802. In this book he described how he'd feel if he discovered a working ticking watch on the ground:

'In crossing a heath, suppose I pitched my foot against a stone and were asked how the stone came to be there; I might possibly answer that, for anything I knew to the contrary, it had lain there for ever: nor would it perhaps be very easy to show the absurdity of this answer. But supposing I had found a watch upon the ground and it should be enquired how the watch happened to be in that place; I should hardly think of the answer which I had given before, that for anything I knew, the watch might always have been there. Yet why should not this answer serve for the watch as well as for the stone?'[11]

He went on to question whether its existence could be explained by the chance forces of wind, rain, heat, and volcanic activity combining together in a billion to one accident, or if it resulted from the deliberate actions of an intelligent watchmaker. He concluded that we should accept the existence of God because of the design seen in creation all around us.

The wonder of it all

While some see aspects of God's design in botany through the lens of a powerful microscope, others trace a sense of creative purpose through the vastness of space though the beam of a radio telescope. Our insignificant Sun is only one of one hundred billion stars swirling around the Milky Way. The Milky Way is so far separated from our neighbouring galaxy Andromeda that it takes light more than two million years to reach us (even though light travels at 186,000 miles per second!)

Is all this just the wonder of 'Nature'? Robert Boyle, the chemist and thermodynamicist, rejected pantheism (seeing God and nature as the same thing) and strongly disapproved of the custom of spelling nature with a capital 'N'. Whilst reflecting on a very intricate clock in Strasbourg, he compared the world's relationship to God with that of a clock to its maker.

Just as the clock-maker had designed and made the clock to run in a regular way, so God has created the world to operate in a uniform way. The clock-maker is distinct from the clock and God is distinct from the Universe itself, for he created it! Boyle pointed to a design above and beyond the physical realm, a design which points to God.

Some quote the thesis of 'evolution' in order to contradict the concept of 'design'. Yet the two theories are not incompatible. There have always been some Christians who have supported Charles Darwin's views expressed in *The Origin* while other Christians have strongly opposed it. Darwin wrote, however, 'in my most extreme fluctuations I have never been an atheist in the sense of denying the existence of a God.'

F R Tennant presented the argument of design in a revised form in 1930. He maintained that belief in God as the Creator is the most plausible argument and used an extended design argument that took Darwin's work into account. Tennant saw the theory of natural selection as being fully in accordance with God's purposes for the Universe. He believed that the whole evolutionary process was the work of God and maintained that God arranged the whole Universe to provide the conditions necessary for life to evolve. Evolution was, he suggested, part of God's plan.

Science is a discipline based on faith. If scientific research does not assume some sense of order in the Universe, the whole scientific process is futile. Imagine a world without the reliable laws of gravity or motion, for example, and the foundation of many scientific theories would be removed.

The development of modern science owes much to Francis Bacon (1561–1626), who believed that God spoke through two 'books', the book of nature and the book of Scripture. He urged those who would understand science to look at the world around them and to study its design, and to read God's word as His revelation to mankind.

If we follow Bacon's advice, the advance of scientific discovery can strengthen rather than weaken our sense of God's involvement in the design of creation. Every new discovery about the mysterious function of the human body, for example, seems to illustrate ever more clearly the awe and wonder we feel in looking at the Universe.

The beauty of order

Although Albert Einstein was not a professing Christian, he recognised aspects of reliable order in the Universe. He wrote: 'To the sphere of religion belongs the faith that the regulations valid for the world of existence are rational, that it is comprehensible to reason. I cannot conceive of a genuine scientist without that profound faith.'

Unless scientists accept the possibility of reason and order in the Universe their discipline can be considered a questionable activity. Einstein continued: 'God is subtle, but He is not malicious. I cannot believe that God plays dice with the Universe. Strenuous intellectual effort and contemplation of God's creation are the angels which will lead me. . .'[12]

John Balchin declared:

'Take a radio telescope and scan the outer reaches of space – or take an electron microscope and explore that hidden world far beyond the range of sight – and everywhere you look you will find order and design. Without it science would be impossible – and life would be intolerable. Everything would be so unsure and uncertain that daily living would be a nightmare. The order, design and law we see in the world tells us that God is not a haphazard, disorganised Creator who either forgets what he has done or who makes things up as he goes along.'[13]

What kind of creator does this sense of order reveal? Albert Einstein concluded that: 'My religion consists of a humble admiration of the illimitable superior Spirit who reveals himself in the slight details we are able to perceive with our frail and feeble minds. That deeply emotional conviction of the presence of a superior reasoning power, which is revealed in the incomprehensible Universe, forms my idea of God.'[14]

As I stood on the 'Salt Sea' of the Sahara and watched the first rays of dawn shining over the horizon I sensed something of the indescribable wonder of creation. As the reds, oranges and yellows of this spectacular dawn reflected from the white landscape all around me the beauty took my breath away.

Perhaps the world's beauty is an accident, perhaps the order is just 'happenstance', and perhaps the intricate way in which it all fits together is just a 'fluke'. Or perhaps, if only we would see it, the cosmos is the evidence we need to lead us to faith in a God of order, design and breathtaking creativity.

The twilight zone!

It was nearly midnight as I walked through the African bush behind the trail of villagers who were my hosts. As part of an experimental youth project I was to stay alone in the mud-hut village, miles out in the bush. I was the first white person they had ever had to stay overnight so far off the beaten track.

The tall man in front of me was carrying my suitcase on his head. At long last we reached the village, where I feasted on lamb's heart, and listened to some of the most joyous singing I had ever heard in my life.

The next day the leader of the community took me for a walk just beyond the village and showed me some big tall trees. 'Before the missionaries came' he said, 'we used to worship the gods in the trees, but through the preachers we discovered the God who made the Universe!'

Travel to any tribe or civilisation on earth and you are likely to discover a sense of 'the divine' and expressions of mankind's deep quest for meaning. Even in our so-called 'secular society' these feelings still find plenty of expression!

When we move at the periphery of rational, emotional and spiritual knowledge we find ourselves in a twilight zone where there are only two options. Eric Jantsch, writing about the 'Self Organising Universe', identifies the two stark alternatives which face those who search for meaning.

'a meaning which can basically never be grasped . . . often expressed in God ideas – and a lack of meaning, which, equally, can never be grasped.'[15]

He calls this longing for meaning the 'moving force of self-transcendence' and speaks of how it reaches out from within us searching for a sense of greater understanding.

The search for meaning

This 'twilight zone' search for meaning surfaces in many different contexts. In North America, for instance, more than 1,200 newspapers carry astrology columns. In the United Kingdom in the mid 1980's a Gallup survey revealed that over 50% of British teenagers said they believed that astrology worked in some form. Ludicrous though it may seem, millions of people turn to astrologers and fortune tellers to make contact with the mystic power of 'destiny'.

Expressions of 'fate', which the advertisers of the British National Lottery have depicted in the form of a finger pointing from the stars, connect with our deepest need for meaning. Nicci Gerrard, writing in *The Observer* about the contemporary addiction to fate, observed that:

> 'We "fall" in love. Then out again. It "was meant". It's not our fault. Madness "descends". Meetings are "meant". Things "turn out" for the best or "just happen". It's a "foregone conclusion". It was in the stars. We grasp at coincidences.'[16]

C G Jung, the eminent psychologist, also recognised our search for meaning. He particularly valued the spiritual, or 'religious' as he called it, aspect of man. Jung suggested that our personal and collective 'unconscious' provides hints about the elements of what man is.

Jung felt that it was particularly important for people in the second half of life to be in touch with a level of unconscious life, to find there a meaning to life and to their lives. This need is not symptomatic of any inadequacy in the person but because it is a reality which is part of balanced mental health and a side to our existence which we avoid at our peril.

We may travel to different civilisations, continents, generations or cultures – but we will find in every time and place a human hunger for spiritual meaning. Our urbanised global village is no exception. Humankind's basic need is to reach out beyond the pressures of everyday life and to sense a greater significance and purpose to their being. A spiritual dimension of life is an important characteristic of being human. Michael and Norrisey observed:

> 'Whenever we touch spiritual values such as love, truth, goodness, beauty, unity, and justice we have had a valid encounter with the reality of God. People speak of such encounters as numinous or transcendent experiences. Our

ability to have such experiences is the meaning of the Biblical expression that we have been made in the image and likeness of God. (Genesis 1:26).'[17]

Some would affirm that the very quality of a person's existence is dependent upon a sensitivity to God. The journalist Malcolm Muggeridge wrote 'When mortal men try to live without God, they infallibly succumb to megalomania or erotomania, or both. The raised fist or the raised phallus: Nietzsche or D H Lawrence. Pascal said this, and the contemporary world bears it out.' [18] .

Is there more to life than death?

Talk to those who have had 'out of the body' experiences in hospital 'trauma units' around the world and you can trace similar patterns of 'God-consciousness' through vivid visions and spiritual experiences. About 20% of those resuscitated talk of an experience of a life beyond death.

Dr Michael Schroeter, a philosopher and neuroscientist at the University of Heidelburg in Germany, believes that the right temporal lobe is where the brain, mind and soul converge in the human body. He believes that the temporal lobe is a receiving system which allows us to hear voices from a source outside our bodies and to see the light that comes to us at the point of death.

Dr Melvin Morse MD has researched near death experiences for many years and is Associate Professor of Paediatrics at the University of Washington. He concludes that: 'The near-death experience probably takes place in the right-temporal lobe, a spot just above the right ear and deep within the brain. Some people think the experience is lessened by showing where it originates in the brain. I disagree. We are talking about the area that houses the very spark of life itself.'[19]

Though some try to explain away such phenomena, it is not so easy to explain the life-transformation that some patients have undergone as a result of near-death experiences. In his remarkable book *Before Death Comes...* Dr Maurice Rawlings, of the Diagnostic Centre in Tennessee describes how he found faith himself as he was resuscitating a man having a 'bad out of body experience' and who pleaded with the doctor to pray for him. He wrote:

> 'Once the pacemaker was in place and the man was taken to the hospital, his condition stabilised. I went home and started reading the Bible to find out what it said about hell. My former belief that death was merely oblivion was being shattered. I was now convinced that there is life after death after all, and that not all of it is good.'

He went on to become a committed Christian, and since then has written extensively on 'out of the body' experiences. Many doctors and nurses who have shared in the final moments of human life talk of the spirit being 'released' and describe experiences of tranquillity when the struggle for life is over and death comes.

What is man?

Observation of animals helps psychologists to understand the animal model, and experimentation with machines enables them to explore the possibilities of artificial intelligence. Both areas of research continue in tandem; but neither model can produce a satisfactory picture of the human spirit as we experience it. These experiments suggest that there is much more to a human life than the sum of chemicals within each person. Such an understanding is at the very foundation of holistic medicine.

Birds can build nests and computers can follow programmes, but human beings have a faculty for creative imagination – for bringing ideas into being – which no animal or machine can imitate. There is a world of difference between animal instinct, computer programmes and the potential of human imagination.[20]

Even Michael Ruse, in his defence of Darwinism, was forced to admit that 'nothing yet even scratches at an explanation of how a transformed ape could produce the magnificence of Beethoven's *Choral Symphony*.'[21]

Humankind has a consciousness of the self – and an ability to transcend beyond the 'I'. We have the ability to ask such questions as 'Who am I?' To our best knowledge, no animal can do such a thing. This aspect of man's psyche is difficult to explain, and indicates that he is clearly different from animals and machines.

The biologist J B S Haldane, who was not writing from a Christian perspective, stated; 'If my mental processes are determined solely by the motions of atoms in my brain, I have no reason to suppose that my beliefs are true ... hence I have no reason to suppose my brain to be composed of atoms.'[22]

There is a general consensus that humankind is unique in creation; and that it expresses a kind of self awareness, ability to decide and creative ability which is far beyond the capability of animals or machines. This sense of the 'I' illustrates the 'multi-layered' complexity of human beings, and marks them out as significant in the purpose of creation. John Polkinghorne wrote:

'Reality is a multi-layered unity. I can perceive another person as an aggregation of atoms, an open biochemical system in interaction with the environment, a specimen of Homo Sapiens, an object of beauty, someone whose needs deserve my respect and compassion, a brother for whom Christ died. All are true and all mysteriously cohere in that one person. To deny one of these levels is to diminish both that person and myself, the perceiver; to do less than justice to the richness of reality. Part of the case for theism is that in God the Creator, the ground of all that is, these different levels find their lodging and their guarantee. He is the source of connection, the one whose creative act holds in one the world views of science, aesthetics, ethics and religion, as expressions of his reason, joy, will and presence.'[23]

We can enter the 'twilight zone' in many different areas of life. In the religious expressions of a tribe in Kenya, in the gypsy fortune-teller's tent at the funfair, or in the 'trauma unit' of a big city hospital. In each context you will find ordinary people reaching out beyond everyday life to seek the supernatural, to discover a 'deeper meaning', or to experience 'something supernatural'.

Christians believe that our search for something beyond 'the twilight zone' is something quite normal and natural. It is a hunger for God which is part of being human. This sense of 'something more' is a symptom of our longing to discover the One who gave us life and in whose plans and purposes alone we can find true meaning.

The 'twilight zone' expresses a longing which can only be fully satisfied when we forge a living relationship with Him, our Creator and our God. In His being we find our true place in the world, and in His love we move out of the 'twilight zone' and 'into the light'.

What place for a Creator?

When the detective visited my home to view the crime-scene, he collected evidence but could not prove who had committed the crime. Anyone who is serious about asking if God is for real would do well to review the evidence. But no one can be argued into the Kingdom of God. That comes through faith, and faith alone!

Stephen Hawking has done the church a favour by putting the age-old question back on the agenda, 'What place, then, for a Creator?' His work has spawned a plethora of new books on this subject.

Don Page lived with Stephen Hawking from 1976 to 1979 while doing his postdoctoral work at Cambridge. He is now a Professor of Physics at the University of Alberta in Edmonton. Don is an evangelical Christian, and he describes how he used to discuss his daily Bible reading with Hawking over breakfast. Reviewing Hawking's question 'What place, then, for a Creator?' and Hawking's concept of time, Page concludes:

'Hawking's new model is more like a circle in which there's not really a beginning or an end. There is in some sense a farthest to the left; so you could say there's something like an earliest time and there's something like a latest time. But in a more technical sense there's no beginning and no end. And yet these both could have been created by God. It's through faith that we can ask the question of whether it (the Universe) was created by God. That is a question which science can neither affirm nor refute.'[24]

God, therefore, cannot be proved. The old French saying *Le Dieu defini c'est Le Dieu fini* (The God defined is the God who is finished) is very appropriate! Yet evidence abounds that this Universe has a purpose, a design, a meaning and a structure. All of these things point to a Creator who holds it all together.

If the scientist prefers to suggest that there is no 'God', no 'Creator', and no 'first cause', what does atheism offer him intellectually? The atheist must, of necessity, believe that matter without mind created reason and logic. Matter without intelligence created understanding and comprehension. Matter without morals created complex ethical codes and legal systems. Matter without conscience created a sense of right and wrong. Matter without emotion created skills in art, music, drama, architecture, language, comedy, literature and dance. Matter without design created in humankind an insatiable hunger for meaning and purpose.

In real terms, atheism is an unsatisfactory position. If the atheist is to be certain that there is no God he must know everything about reality. He must know all facts and truth of existence. He must possess infinite knowledge throughout time, be everywhere at the same time, and be absolutely sure of everything. In reality, the atheist must be omniscient, omnipresent, and omnipotent. Atheism is a universal negative, and therefore impossible to prove. It is little wonder, therefore, that many claim that it takes more faith to be an atheist than to believe in God.

When I was sixteen years of age I attended an Easter youth

camp which was being held in beautiful Worcestershire countryside. One clear spring night, after a rather riotous barbecue, I lay on the ground and looked into the starlit sky. The bonfire was burning low and the air was still and clear. As I looked up into the sky and focused on the galaxy of stars reaching out into infinity I wondered what was behind it all, and why it all existed.

That night was an important marker on my spiritual pilgrimage – for it was the beginning of my search for God. I can well remember my youth leader saying, 'Start with the miracle, the miracle that made everything happen . . . and begin to ask who or what the miracle is.'

Although I was neither a scientist nor a philosopher, I began to look seriously for a 'theory of everything', a 'first cause', and an 'explanation of the miracle'. I remember walking into the wood and praying, *Dear God, I'm not sure I can believe it all or accept it all, but if you're real – be real to me.*

There was no bright light, no booming voice from the night sky, and no sense of having 'found God'. But something had changed within me, I had moved from being an atheist to being a 'seeker after God'. I had moved from sarcasm to openness, and I had moved from escapism to a recognition of my longing for God.

Over the following year I explored many ideas, discussed many possibilities, and began to read the story of Jesus. As I grasped the idea of a creative intelligence behind the world my life began to make more sense to me. And when I came to accept that this Creator loved what he had made, and loved it so much that he became incarnate within it in through Jesus Christ. . . . I found that the Christian message really made sense.

Twelve months later I went back to the same camp, found the same tree in the wood, and prayed a prayer of faith. I gave my life to God. I placed my own broken and disordered life within the order and purposes of the Creator. I discovered that there is a designer, there is a plan and there is hope!

I found in him the One on whom all things depend. He is the source of meaning, life and direction for which I had longed. In his power my life became ordered and empowered. In his love I found forgiveness, healing and connection. I found life which nothing else could have given me. I moved out of the twilight zone and into the light!

3

'Isn't Science About Proof, While Christianity Is About Faith?'

(David Wilkinson)

'Science gives us proof, while religion is just about faith' is a comment often heard in the discussion of science and Christianity, both at the popular level and sometimes at the academic level. It is a view that is based on years of supposed conflict between science and Christianity and often reinforced by media images. But is it true?

To boldly go ... science or religion?

The man who has shaped many people's view of late twenti-eth-century science was not a scientist at all. Gene Roddenberry, the creator of *Star Trek*, dreamed his science fiction in the midst of American scientific optimism which culminated in NASA's success of putting a man on the moon and returning him safely to the Earth. The first showing of *Star Trek* did not prove to be so popular, but since then it has achieved cult status and Hollywood popularity. At some time, somewhere in the world, on 365 days a year *Star Trek* is being shown. Concepts such as 'beam me up Scottie', 'warp drive' and 'dilithium crystals' are for many people an accurate description of the future!

Perhaps more importantly, Roddenberry's view of the nature of science epitomises what most people think. Science is logical and is all conquering. The science officer of the original series is Mr Spock, half human and half Vulcan, devoted to logic. In *Star Trek: The Next Generation*, the science officer on the USS *Enterprise* is a character called Mr Data. If Spock had been devoted to logic while resisting his human emotion, Data on the face of it has no such problem. He is a walking computer, an android who is able to analyse a situation and come up with the solution. He is the ultimate stereotype of science.

In Mr Data, science is represented by a cool collecting of facts (data), and then these facts being fed into a computer program, governed by the rules of logic, which gives the answer. Science can only give an incorrect answer if it doesn't have enough data or if the computer goes wrong. If neither of these things happen, then Mr Data always gives us proof. Indeed, some would argue, such a simple method is capable of being applied to all questions in the Universe.

Of course computers can go wrong. Recently, the manufacturer Intel agreed to replace the millions of chips in Pentium computers that were found to make mistakes in some mathematical calculations. The inevitable joke was, 'How do you use a Pentium machine so that you get the correct mathematical answer?' 'Steady your hand against it so you don't shake your slide rule!'

Nevertheless, the popular image of science remains. It delivers! After all, the very fact that I am writing this on a computer, while in the background I hear the sound of the television from another room, cars on the street outside and a helicopter overhead is testimony enough, never mind our ability to send humans into space, to probe the structure of DNA and tell the story of the early Universe.

As a young research student I remember visiting a colleague in India. As he drove me from the airport, we passed men, women and children on the streets of Bombay, living, begging and dying. We then turned into Homi Bhabha Road, where at the end stood a huge white building, surrounded by its manicured grounds and security fences. We were going to Tata Institute of Fundamental Research. There on the outskirts of the human misery of much of Bombay, we would work in a government institution with over 100 professors of physics, state of the art computing and even a western cafeteria for the visiting scientists. I eventually asked my colleague how this was politically justified. The reply was that in the creation of independent India, science was highly valued. Nehru commenting on the problems facing the nation such as poverty, hunger, and justice said, 'It is science alone that can solve the problems....The future belongs to science and those who make friends with science'[25]

Now of course much has changed in terms of people's confidence in science to shape society for the good. I write this on the 50th anniversary of the day that the US bomber *Enola Gay* dropped 'Little Boy'. At 8.15 am, when the device was 2,500ft above the ground, conventional explosives triggered runaway nuclear fission in the uranium core. The result was that at least 70,000 people died instantly in the Japanese city of Hiroshima. This triumph for the scientists and engineers of the Manhattan Project led to death, destruction, leukaemia, abortions and eventually the cold war, deterrents, and the prospect of nuclear winters. We may no longer fear nuclear Armageddon, but we still face the proliferation of weapons and a clutch of issues concerning nuclear power. Day by day we continue to pollute the environment and use valuable resources. The Parthenon has suffered more damage in the last forty years than in the other 2350 years of its existence, due to the chemicals we pump 'scientifically' into the atmosphere. In the same way genetic engineering, the use of animals for scientific research, and some modern medical treatments all raise difficult and often frightening moral questions. The following words sum it up:

'No one, not even the most brilliant scientist alive today knows where science is taking us. We are aboard a train that is gathering speed, racing down a track on which there are an unknown number of switches leading to unknown destinations. No single scientist is in the engine cab and there may be demons at the wheel.'[26]

But we are going down the track because science is so successful in achieving its aim of understanding and manipulating the natural order of the Universe.

All of this is in stark contrast with the popular image of religion. If science is hurtling down the track, religion is often seen as going for a pleasant afternoon stroll, taking a break from the real world and eventually getting lost because of uncertainty and nice platitudes! The religious believer, it is claimed, pays no regard to evidence, but has 'blind faith' in the sense of the old schoolboy definition of faith 'is believing things you know aren't true'. The biologist Lewis Wolpert wrote,' Science tries to understand how the world works and is constantly tested against reality. . . . By contrast, religion is largely based on unquestioning certainties.'[27] If religious believers, he seems to imply, do not show such dogmatic faith, then they have total uncertainty about everything.

Furthermore, there are those who doubt the very validity of theology itself. Richard Dawkins, the Oxford zoologist and populariser of science, said in his own characteristic style, 'What has "theology" ever said that is of the smallest use to anybody? When has "theology" ever said anything that is demonstrably true and is not obvious?'[28] When Susan Howatch, the best selling author, recently donated £1 million to establish the Starbridge Lectureship in Science and Religion at Cambridge University, the editorial in the premier scientific journal *Nature* criticised the move on the basis that science was a worthy academic subject but theology was not.

If the popular view of religion was to be incorporated into *Star Trek*, the character would not be called Mr Data but probably Mrs 'Unsure why I believe and good for nothing'! And it is very clear which character you would want on board your USS *Enterprise* if the Romulans attacked. Norman Vincent Peale told the story of being on an aircraft when the voice of the Captain said, 'We need to inform you that one of our engines has shut down, but the other three will enable us to complete our journey'. He then added, 'To reassure any of you who might be worried, let me tell you that we have four

Methodist bishops on board today'. A woman beside Peale called a stewardess and said, 'Could you please tell the Captain, with respect, I'd be far happier if there were three bishops and four engines.' The provable certainty of science is contrasted to the dogmatic obscurantism or naive uncertainty of religion. In finding out about the world then it is clear which is the most trustworthy.

Such a contrast however is grossly misleading. It does not do justice to either the complexity of science and theology, or to the fact that they have much in common.

How do we know what we think we know?

To understand this more, we need to address the question of how do we know what we think we know, or as philosophers would call it the question of epistemology. This is not as easy as it may first appear. Bertrand Russell put it starkly:

> 'we have to ask ourselves whether, in any sense at all, there is such a thing as matter. Is there a table which has a certain intrinsic nature, and continues to exist when I am not looking, or is the table merely a product of my imagination, a dream table in a very prolonged dream? The question is of the greatest importance. For if we cannot be sure of the independent existence of objects, we cannot be sure of the independent existence of other people's bodies, and there-fore still less of other people's minds, since we have no grounds for believing in their minds except such as are derived from observing their bodies. Thus if we cannot be sure of the independent existence of objects we shall be left alone in a desert – it may be that the whole outer world is nothing but a dream and that we alone exist.'[29]

Now you might say that such thoughts are inevitable from professional philosophers who have nothing better to do than stare at tables! But it is a fundamental question for science and religion. I once saw some graffiti scrawled upon a philos-ophy department notice board:

What is matter? – never mind
What is mind? – it doesn't matter!

But in the end it does matter. When scientists say that tables are made of atoms, and atoms are made of protons, neutrons and electrons, is it true or is it all made up? When Christians talk about a relationship with God, is God really there or are they simply deluding themselves? How do we know and is the way of knowing different between science and religion? Is one better than the other?

The famous American physicist Richard Feynman used to tell the story of how as a child his father would take him for walks in the woods and talk to him about nature. After one of these walks, a child said to Feynman, 'You see that bird up there in the tree. What is it called?' Feynman confessed that he did not know and the child mocked him. Upset, Feynman went to his father and asked him why he had not told him the name of the bird. His father then told him what the bird was called in English, in French, in German and in a whole host of other languages. He then said to Feynman that he could know the name of the bird but that would not mean that he would understand it, its nesting habits, its feeding, and many other things. To know how to label things is not primarily how to understand them.

Both science and religion claim not just to label the world but to attempt to understand it. We need to be clear on how they do that and what they actually achieve. We will take science first and then contrast it with theology.

How do you do science?

If you were to be introduced to a scientist what would you expect? Someone whose knees were dirty from crawling through undergrowth to collect frogs, or someone with a head twice the size of a normal head who spent the evening writing down mathematical equations? Such are popular views of science but neither by itself is correct.

By reason alone?

In a wood on Christmas Eve 1938, sitting on a tree trunk, Lise Meitner and her nephew Otto Frisch, discussed a letter from her colleague Otto Hahn. Hahn had found that if uranium was bombarded with neutrons, then it seemed to break up to produce barium. The letter asked, 'Perhaps you can put forward some fantastic explanation?' On the back of Hahn's letter they wrote down the consequences. If the uranium atom split into two atoms of barium, then the process would produce energy, nuclear energy.

That picture of scientists sitting in a wood, thinking and putting their thoughts onto 'the back of an envelope' is a typical picture. The cover of the best selling *A Brief History of Time,* has a picture of Professor Stephen Hawking in front of a blackboard with a number of mathematical equations on it. It gives the impression that our understanding of the origin of the Universe comes just from a blackboard and a great thinker. Such an impression is not, however, the whole picture.

In some ways such a view is a legacy of the dominant aspects of Greek science. The foundations of science forged in the Greek culture were the use of mathematics and the belief that science was a rational exercise. Such foundations form the basis of modern science, but within Greek culture they were pushed to the limits. The philosopher Plato laughed at astronomers who expected to find truth from observing the heavens. Why? Because the nature of the Universe could be deduced from logic. All you needed was one or two starting points, an understanding of logic and mathematics and on the back of your papyrus you could find out all that could be known about the Universe.

This tradition found its fullest expression in the rationalism of the French philosopher René Descartes in the seventeenth century. Descartes spent much of his life joining armies but making sure he stayed away from the fighting. He then became private tutor to Queen Christina of Sweden. However, his most important contribution was a breakthrough which transformed western philosophy. In the winter of 1619–20 he recorded how he 'entered a stove' and spent the day in meditation. It is generally held that what he meant was that he entered a room with a stove in it, although there are a lot of jokes about his philosophy being half-baked or brittle around the edges! Searching for a reliable way of knowing about the world he started to doubt everything. He was finally pushed to the conclusion that the only thing he could not doubt, was that he was doubting. His starting point was 'I think therefore I am' and from that 'sure' starting point with reliable logic he constructed his understanding of God, the Universe and everything.

The trouble with this approach is that it is actually not very productive. Sometimes these days I receive papers and manuscripts on 'new' theories of the Universe. I once received a manuscript of 300 hand-written pages detailing such a theory. With great care and logic the author had tried to explain the existence, evolution and structure of the Universe from the starting point that at the heart of the Universe were perfect spheres. However, logical his theory was, I am afraid it just did not work, for his starting point was all wrong. His theory had been worked out with no reference to the real world around. The story goes of a mathematician who was asked to help the Milk Marketing Board improve the efficiency of milk production. After many months of work, he sent in his report worked out in fine detail. However, it began with the words, 'Consider a spherical cow . . .' We might like the world to be simple but it is often far more complicated!

Now of course, science is an activity of reason. It is rational but not rationalistic. That means it does not proceed by reason alone. Anyone can sit down with logic and the back of an envelope but they will not be a scientist.

By data alone?

An opposite view is that science proceeds by data alone. Archimedes sits in his bath and instead of playing with his rubber duck, sees the displacement of bath water and immediately shouts 'Eureka, I've found a new scientific law!' This view says that as long as you collect enough data or observations of the world you will understand the world.

In 1610 Galileo was the first to point his telescope skywards rather than at other nation's ships. He saw what appeared to be some bright stars around the planet Jupiter, and after many nights of observation concluded that they revolved around Jupiter. What he had seen were four of the moons of Jupiter. In many books, you will then read a sentence something like, 'this proved the Copernican theory that the Earth revolved around the Sun, and that the earth was not the centre of the Universe'. Now there is some truth in this, but at face value it is very misleading. It is as if the light from Jupiter's moon came into Galileo's telescope and out the other end came proof that the Sun was at the centre of the Solar System of planets.

As you might expect the story was a little more complicated than that. Galileo published his findings in a book *The Starry Messengers*. This in itself did not show very much. However, later Galileo saw that Venus, just like the Moon, had phases, that is sometimes you could see all of it and other times only part of it. This would happen if Venus went around the Sun. So Galileo first had seen moons going around Jupiter. This told him simply that all bodies in the Solar System did not orbit the Earth and by analogy one could think of the Earth orbiting the Sun. Second, he had seen the phases of Venus. But even these two observations in themselves did not inevitably lead to the understanding that the Sun was at the centre of the Solar System.

Galileo had to argue the case. In 1611 he visited Rome where he debated with the astronomers of the Jesuit Roman College. Contrary to the popular myth, this was not a 'conflict' between science and religion but a battle between different scientific theories. For almost 1500 years the view of Ptolemy, a Greek astronomer, had put the Earth at the centre of the Universe. It pictured the heavenly bodies as moving in perfect circles around the Earth. However, the planets did not follow this pattern. By introducing epicycles (a second circle added with its centre moving around the main circle) you could explain this motion, but some eighty circles were needed in all. This made it very complicated!

Now, as the astronomers of Roman College eventually acknowledged, Galileo's observations of the phases of Venus did disprove the picture of Ptolemy. But what was to replace it? There were already a few candidates around. Copernicus' *On the Revolutions of the Heavenly Spheres* was published in 1543, and gave a rival picture to Ptolemy. However, his system was not particularly simple either. Although the Sun was at the centre, in his calculations the planets rotate about the centre of the Earth's orbit which was not the same as the position of the Sun. As it happens, Copernicus needed as many epicycles as Ptolemy to explain the motion of the planets. To further complicate the matter, Venus's phases also fitted with the theory of another astronomer, Tycho Brahe, in which the planets orbited the Sun but the Sun in turn orbited the Earth.

In fact, it was only when Kepler in 1609 dispensed with circular motion of the planets and suggested that the planets move in ellipses that epicycles were no longer needed and the observations were fully explained. The real evidence that the Sun was at the centre of the Solar System had to wait until 1838 for F W Bessel's observation of the way the Earth moves in relation to the other stars.

Nevertheless, at this stage Galileo was welcomed by Rome and as many historians have pointed out it was Galileo himself who seemed to go out of his way to manufacture trouble, even indulging in a bitter attack on a Jesuit who disagreed with him, who would later be Commissary General at Galileo's trial at the Inquisition!

The Galileo 'affair' is not a story of the clash of science and religion. There were theological disputes on how to interpret the Bible and the authority of the church, but some of the theologians were with Galileo. Some have suggested that if Galileo had not been so aggressive, there may not have been an 'affair' at all.

What the story does illustrate however is how messy science

is. It is a very complicated business proceeding by neither data or reason alone. It involves personalities, power struggles, competing theories, limited data and judgements that need to be made. This always needs to be remembered when we hear phrases such as 'scientists say' or 'science has proved'.

There's more to this than meets the eye!

In science there is always an interplay going on between theory and experiment. It is true that modern science places a high emphasis on observation, but that in itself is never enough. For example, there are often disagreements on the observations. A modern example is whether a particle called the neutrino has mass. Neutrinos were discovered in 1956 and they fill the whole Universe. In fact as you read this sentence many will be passing through your head. In 1981 observations from a Russian experiment suggested that the neutrino particle had a very small mass. However, other experiments have collected data that the neutrino is of zero mass.

Now you might think this is not very important. In fact it is very important for what scientists currently believe will be the future of the Universe. As we shall see in Chapter Five, observations suggest that our Universe is expanding, that is the space between the galaxies is getting larger. Looking forward, the question is, will it expand for ever? If the neutrino does have mass then gravity would be strong enough to slow and even reverse the expansion, leading to the Universe collapsing back on itself. Now this may not be a great practical question, as such a collapse would happen in some billions of years in the future! However, such an important question about the way the world is depends on agreement on the data, which has not yet been achieved.

We might also point out that all observations are to some extent dependent on theory. Very rarely today will anyone do a 'Galileo' and simply point a telescope at the sky and collect observations. Science is carried out by real people with their own thoughts, preferences and prejudices. It is also carried out in a scientific and political community which apportions money to do experiments. To apply for a research grant you need to have some theory in mind about which data to collect. You cannot request time to use the Hubble Space Telescope to simply 'point it out at space and see what we get'! It must be for some purpose which includes how important a research proposal is to our total understanding of the Universe. You need a bit of theory first, which you will then test with observations. The observations may then cause you to modify the theory, and so on.

What then makes a good theory? First and foremost it is whether the observations fit. Ptolemy's theory could not encompass Galileo's observation of the phases of Venus. However, there are other criteria too. These things are needed to decide between two competing theories, both of which might be supported by the observations. Scientists talk of good theories in terms of:

- whether they are consistent with the observations
- whether they can predict accurately
- whether they are elegant
- whether they are able to unify our understanding of different aspects of the physical world

In all of these things, judgements are involved on the part of the scientist. They are judging what is worth doing, and deciding which is the better theory. Some philosophers of science talk about the making of these judgements as 'skills' as a way of pointing out that it is something that scientists can develop with experience, but cannot be precisely written down in a textbook.

In addition, there is a further problem. It is that science always draws general conclusions from particular instances. If you observe that in particular regions of the Galaxy, stars form out of massive clouds of molecular hydrogen gas, it is unrealistic to go on to say, 'Until I have looked at every such region in the whole of the Universe I will not believe that stars form out of molecular hydrogen.' At some point you need to make a judgement on the amount of evidence you have. That is the principle of induction. Your theory cannot be proved as you would have to test all occurrences everywhere. In the light of this, the philosopher Sir Karl Popper proposed that a theory cannot be verified but can only be falsified. If you saw one occurrence which falsified your theory that would be enough. This is nice philosophically but is very difficult in practice. In fact science does not proceed in this way. Once again scientists use their judgement to decide what is an appropriate amount of evidence, while always being ready to have the theory changed by new observations.

Finally, there is the element to science of creative imagination. Einstein's revolution of physics through his theories of relativity leading to the famous equation $E = mc^2$ was in large part due to extraordinary 'intuition'. The chemist Kekule was trying to figure out the molecular structure that would explain the properties of benzene. In a dream he saw a snake grasp its tail in its mouth. When he awoke he realised that a closed ring of carbon atoms would explain the properties. This was supported by further experimentation. Now these major breakthroughs may only happen rarely. A friend once said to Einstein, 'When I have a good idea, I do not want to forget it, so I keep a notebook by my bed. What do you do?' Einstein replied, 'I do not understand your question. I have only had two or three good ideas in my life!'

The result of all of this is that computers cannot do science! Mr Data of *Star Trek* is more fiction than science. There was once a survey on accidents in the home which concluded that 90% of accidents on the stairs involved the top or bottom stairs. The data was fed into a computer in order to find out how accidents could be reduced. The answer came back 'remove the top and bottom stairs'!

Science is rational but not like a computer program. It is not as if in a book like this we can write out the way to do science. There are proper procedures such as the collection of observations, the testing of theories with certain criteria, but there is the important role of the scientist. Our knowledge of the world through science involves real people using judgements and intuition in the interplay of theory and observations.

Of course this does not mean that science is a highly individualistic activity where anything goes. The role of the scientific community is very important. Theories need to be published in journals or conferences where they will be scrutinised both before and after publication by one's colleagues. Experiments will be conducted by others to test the validity of the claims of any new theory.

A few years ago Martin Fleischmann and Stanley Pons gave a news conference where they claimed that they had seen 'cold fusion' in a test tube. Nuclear fusion is the energy source of stars and if we were able to produce and control it, we would solve the world's energy problems in a flash. However, this fusion process was believed only to occur at the very high temperatures and pressures within a star. Fleischmann and Pons claimed that they had produced it in a cold test tube in a chemistry lab!

Even while the newspapers were awash with these claims, other scientists were already trying to recreate their experiment to check it, while others were attempting to understand the theory behind their claims. Evidence could not be provided to support their 'breakthrough', and on the basis of that the scientific community refused to accept it. Only those things which are generally accepted will then be taught to the next generation. Thus the scientific community together limits and re-enforces an individual judgement.

So what does science achieve?

Science uses observations of the world to look for patterns by which the complexity of the Universe can be understood. But do those patterns tell us what the world is really like? A number of views exist on this.

1. What a perfect photograph!

Most scientists themselves view science in terms of 'naive realism'. That is they tend to believe that scientific theories give an accurate description of the world as it is in itself. If you like, a theory is like a photograph, giving an exact representation of reality.

The difficulty with such a view however is why are previous 'photographs' different from the one we have now. Presumably if we were living at the time of Ptolemy, we would believe that the Earth actually was at the centre of the Universe. We now know that such a view is wrong. It wasn't a perfect photograph after all. Theories change and in the light of history it would be foolish to say that the present theories we now have are the perfect representations of reality. They are simply the best we have at the moment.

2. It just gives you the information to do things

As a child, I was always amazed to think that London had been laid out in such straight lines. I found it incredible that South Kensington, Victoria, Westminster and Embankment stations all lay in a horizontal line west to east, and that London Bridge and Morden were linked by a straight line at forty-five degrees which perfectly ran through fourteen other parts of London. Of course my view of London was based on the Underground map, and as I later realised it was not really like that! The map is arranged in that kind of way to make it easy for the traveller to identify stations and routes in order to get where they want to go, rather than giving a geography of the capital city.

Many people, especially technologists and engineers view science in this way. They view scientific theories just as calculating devices in order to do things, simply giving us a handle on the world. In fact when Copernicus suggested his theory that the Sun did not revolve around the Earth, a Lutheran minister, Andreas Osiander, advised him to publish it as a convenient calculating device for predicting more accurately the movement of the planets, rather than a theory which told us about reality. Although Copernicus was not convinced by this, Osiander wrote an anonymous preface to the book in which he claimed that the theory was not true but just a correct basis for calculation. In doing this Osiander thought that opposition to the theory might be minimised.

Such a view has something to be said for it. Science does give us a handle on the world to do things. This can be a benefit when confronted with theories like quantum mechanics. Physicists disagree on what this theory actually tells about reality, but it does work, giving us amongst many other things lasers and nuclear power.

However, even if it allows us to do things which we do not fully understand at the moment, we still want to understand. John Polkinghorne illustrates with a striking parable. Suppose a black box was delivered to the Meteorological Office, which when you fed in today's weather would enable scientists to predict the weather exactly for the next year. No one would complain about forecasters getting the weather wrong, but the scientists would not be satisfied. They would want to know what was in the box and how it was able to make such accurate predictions. We want to understand for understanding's sake as well as know how to use it.

3. It's just all in the mind

Have you ever had a dream so vivid that you cannot tell whether it was really a dream or whether it really happened? Did it just go on in your mind, as a result of wishes, memories and the need to cope with the world, or was there really something there?

Some philosophers have suggested a similar thing with science. It is as if science does not give us a photograph of reality but is a photograph of what we have just dreamt up in our minds. The view comes from the philosophy of Immanuel Kant and is commonly called idealism. It sees the scientific laws as a description not of the world outside of us, but a description of the way our minds organise the data from our senses. Thus, order does not exist in nature but is imposed onto nature by our minds. Science does not give us knowledge of the world in itself, rather it shows us how our minds work.

On this view, if we say that a table is made up of atoms, we are not saying that there are atoms really there. All we are doing is constructing an easy way to talk about what tables are made of. To push this to its logical conclusion it would mean that atoms did not 'exist' until their discovery. Sir Arthur Eddington used the illustration of fishing. Send a young scientist out on a fishing boat, asking them to bring back a report on the size of fish. So the scientist waits until the catch is brought in, and with great care measures each fish. However, he makes a startling conclusion. He finds that there are no fish at all smaller than four inches! He is about to write his famous paper on *The discovery that there are no small fish in the ocean*, when a wise old fisherman tells him to look at the nets. The nets have four-inch holes, so it is not surprising that in this catch you do not see fish in the ocean smaller than four inches. By the nature of the way you have examined the world, you have imposed such an order.

Such anti-realist views, that is saying that science does not tell us about the world in itself, have become popular particularly amongst *philosophers* of science. This is due no doubt to the experience that theories do change and the importance of personal judgements in the method of science. However, they are not popular amongst *scientists*. It may sit conveniently in a philosophy textbook but it does not reflect the reality of a scientific laboratory. The astrophysicist John Barrow calls it a fashionable but ill fitting glove. It is ill fitting for a number of reasons:

The success of science If science is just constructed by our minds why is it so successful? Max Perutz, the Nobel prize winning molecular biologist writes, 'The bulk of scientific knowledge is final. If it were not, jet planes could not fly, computers would not work and atom bombs would fail to explode'[30] That is if I am in a plane travelling along a runway with sea ahead, I want to know that the design of the wings is based on an understanding of what is really there, rather than just how an engineer's mind works! Science is successful because it discovers what is really there.

The effort of science   Why do we as a society spend so much time, effort and money on the scientific enterprise? We could replace the telescopes, the particles colliders, laboratories and scientists costing billions of dollars worldwide, with a few cheap psychologists who would tell us how our minds work!

The nature of science   Such a view of science inevitably falls into its own trap. If science is simply constructed by our own minds, then the statement 'science is simply constructed by our own minds' is also simply constructed by our own minds, and if that is the case why believe it as true!

The continuity of science   Theories do change but it would be a wrong view of science to think that there is no common ground between successive theories. When Albert Einstein devised his theories of motion and gravitation (the Special and General Theories of Relativity) they replaced Isaac Newton's earlier theories. Some have talked of this as a major 'revolution' where one theory has given us a totally new picture of the Universe. However, although Einstein's theories were more comprehensive in explaining phenomena in the Universe such as black holes and the relationship between time and space, they had to be consistent with Newton's theories at an everyday level (i.e. at speeds much less than the speed of light). Even major 'revolutions' of theories have an element of continuity, suggesting that we are getting a fuller and more accurate picture of the world.

The surprises of science   Finally scientists know the experience of reality poking its head through our often overly rigid ideas. J B S Haldane once said, 'My suspicion is that the

Universe is not only queerer than we suppose, but queerer than we can suppose'. In that he was right, as any scientist who researches or teaches will know. The concepts within theories such as quantum theory or relativity are totally outside our common sense or ability to fully understand. They involve for example:

- particles which are in many places at the same time
- as a spaceship speeds up close to the speed of light it increases in mass and the time measured on board runs slower compared to clocks back on earth
- some fifteen billion years ago the whole Universe was smaller than the eye of a needle

These are staggering concepts. All have come through our exploration of the world around us, in ways which have challenged our own expectations. In research there is a real feeling of discovery and indeed surprise that often the world is far simpler and more subtle than expected.

4. Improving the picture!

There is a way of holding together all of the above insights. That is, the impression of science making genuine discoveries about the world, the acknowledgement of the part played by scientists and the provisional nature of scientific theories. Such a view is called 'critical realism'. It says that science gives us a tightening grip on reality.

Science is not an exact photograph, or a self portrait. It is perhaps more like a drawing or painting of a scene which is being constantly improved as more is observed. Or it could be likened not to an underground map, but to the work of a map maker who fills in more and more details on the map of what is actually there. As his knowledge grows, so more of the map is filled in. Sometimes mistakes are made which give a misleading picture. These have to be corrected as the map is checked more and more.

This view takes seriously what our observations do tell us

of reality. There is something 'out there', and science discovers it. However, it says that our description of reality may not be in naive everyday terms, and that there is a significant personal role in the method of science. Some say that scientific theories exhibit 'verisimilitude', that is they are 'very similar to' reality but not absolute truth. They are only partial and provisional ways of describing reality. As more data is gathered, theories will be modified leading us closer to reality. I suggest that this view of science may not be the most simple and elegant in philosophical terms but is the most true to its nature. It questions the view that science ever gives us a total and finished picture of the world.

The great British astronomer Sir Arthur Eddington once stated that there are 15,747,724,136,275,002,577,605,653,961, 181,55,468,044,717,914,527,116,709,366,231,425,076,185,631, 031,296 protons in the Universe and the same number of electrons. He was wrong! The scientist should be a little more hesitant. In terms of the popular view of things, science does not 'prove things'. Science proceeds on the gathering of evidence and then judgements made on the weighing of that evidence.

So it is time to go back to one of our original questions. How do we know what we think we know in science? Let me suggest a definition. Science is a 'subtle interplay of experience and interpretation involving personal judgements within a committed community exploring an objective reality'. It does not give absolute proof or a total and finished picture of the world. It is not something that can be done by computers but is a human activity.

What are the limits of science?

'Someday, science may be able to explain why a child can't walk around a puddle!' This may be sarcastic but the person who said it is reacting to the notion that science is all conquering. Is there anything outside the ability of science to answer?

For some, if science cannot give the answer then it is a non-question. Bertrand Russell wrote, 'Whatever knowledge is attainable, must be attained by scientific means; and what science cannot discover, mankind cannot know'[31] Richard Dawkins[32] put it more simply, 'Truth means scientific truth', making science the ultimate test of what to believe. Instead of science, I suggest this is 'scientism'.

This view has been around since the early years of this century. It comes from a philosophy called logical positivism. It dismissed all moral or theological statements as meaningless because they could not be proved by direct observation. This led to science being seen as the only true source of knowledge of the world, everything else is 'pie in the sky when you die'. It also underlies the belief that the existence of God is not meaningful unless you can find some sort of scientific test.

However, there are two major problems. First, what does it say about science? Science is based on certain assumptions which cannot be proved by direct observation. One of these assumptions, is that although the Universe changes, the underlying laws are the same at all times and places. These have to be accepted for science to begin. And if you cannot prove these then science, which is the only source of true knowledge, is actually not true knowledge!

Second, what is the status of the statement that 'only those things which could be proved by direct observation are meaningful'. It is neither true by definition nor could be proved by direct observation! It was meaningless in its own terms! Like the Babel fish 'disproof' of God in *The Hitchhikers Guide to the Galaxy*, this view should disappear in a puff of its own logic!

Yet today, many still make the mistake of applying science to all questions of the Universe, including morality and purpose. It is often because of the great success of science in exploiting and understanding the world, that scientists have become blind to the limits of their subject. They have given the popular impression that anything can be believed if announced in the name of science. Perhaps they have been encouraged by the fact that scientists specialise so early, which means that they are often have quite a narrow view of the world, becoming critical of other disciplines. The great physicist Lord Rutherford echoed such criticism when he said, 'science is physics and stamp collecting'.

Donald MacKay, who was an internationally respected scientist researching the human brain, coined the phrase 'nothing buttery' for the view that science can answer everything and what science cannot answer is worthless. It is the attitude that says that something is nothing but the scientific description of it. People fall into this trap all of the time, for example when they say that human beings are 'nothing but' atoms and molecules. Of course human beings are made of atoms and molecules. But it is a major mistake to then say we are nothing but that.

One may say that a record of Bob Seeger's *Even now* is nothing but grooves of varying width on a circular piece of vinyl! That is a scientific description but there is a lot more to it than that. The way the grooves are positioned interact with the stylus to produce sound. The sound is made of notes of music, but it is only when you take them as a whole and in the right order that they are heard as a rock tune. The lyrics are individual words which when taken together communicate story, images and sentiments. These things are dependent on the grooves, but cannot be fully explained just by the grooves. A physicist can explain how the sound is produced, but they need musicians to understand the music. Even then, that's not the full story. For that record holds a special meaning within my relationship with my wife. This meaning cannot be understood from the lyrics alone, for it depends on the lyrics in relation to our own history.

As a physics student, I was rather arrogant. I thought that everything would be explained by physics as everything was made up of atoms and molecules. Thus, chemistry was for those who could not do physics, biology for those who could not do chemistry, psychology for those who could not do biology, and sociology for those who could do nothing else! I know now how wrong I was!

When atoms and molecules get together in gases, liquids and solids they exhibit properties which cannot be explained by just an understanding of atoms. They possess emergent properties such as wetness and colour. These things are not possessed by the atoms themselves. You need chemists who study these combinations. Life is when certain chemicals combine in a particular way. Water itself does not possess 'life', but is an important part of any living thing. Biologists are needed to study the emergent properties of living things. Living things range from simple forms like the amoeba to complex creatures like human beings. Above certain levels of complexity, new properties emerge such as consciousness, self awareness, guilt and understanding. Enter psychologists! And when these human beings interact with one another, there's even a place for sociologists!

Within science itself we need to be clear that one discipline has not got all the answers. On the basis of this we should not be surprised that there are many questions which are beyond the reach of science. 'Scientism' does not stand up to scrutiny and there are many who acknowledge this. The journalist Brian Appleyard wrote, 'Science begins by saying it can answer only *this* kind of question and ends by claiming that *these* are the only questions that can be asked'[33] Erwin Schrödinger, famous for his work on quantum theory said, 'I am very astonished that the scientific picture of the real world around me is very deficient. It gives a lot of factual information, puts all our experience in a magnificently consistent order, but it is ghastly silent about all and sundry that is really near to our heart . . . it knows nothing of beautiful and ugly, good or bad, God and eternity. Science sometimes pretends to answer questions in these domains, but the answers are very often so silly that we are not inclined to take them seriously'[34]

Peter Medawar, Nobel Laureate and often fierce critic of religion, nevertheless acknowledged, 'That there is indeed a limit upon science is made very likely by the existence of questions that science cannot answer and that no conceivable advances of science would empower it to answer. These are the questions that children ask – the 'ultimate questions' of Karl Popper. I have in mind such questions as:

How did everything begin?
What are we all here for?
What is the point of living?'[35]

Science is a successful activity because it does limit the questions that it addresses to the world. Its methods do not answer questions of value, beauty, purpose or as Tolstoy put it, science 'does not tell us how to live'.

In fact some have not just questioned scientism, they have rejected science itself. This is especially true in certain strands of the New Age movement. The New Age is a term which ties together certain groups and individuals. Common to it is putting intuition above intellect, and feeling above theory, in reaction to the rather arrogant claims and stale rationalism of what is perceived to be modern science. So one of its leading proponents, Gary Zukav states, 'We are approaching the end of science'[36]. What he means by that, is not that science will be abolished, but that science cannot answer all of the questions and the role of intuition needs to be heightened.

What these New Age writers are doing is that they are criticising scientism, but the mistake they make is to go on and reject science itself. Archimedes is being thrown out with the bath water! While Christians may agree that science is wrong to claim to answer all of the questions, Christians will acknowledge that science itself is part of God's gift in creation.

What is the Christian understanding of science?

Imagine a Christian who is a scientist working in a laboratory doing research on the udder of a cow (as a friend of mine once did!). Apart from having some interesting dinner conversation, we might ask whether there would be anything different about her science because of her Christian faith. Will her faith affect her science? The answer is yes and no.

1. A common method

In terms of day to day science, her scientific method will be the same as that practised by colleagues of other faiths or none. All will be committed to the subtle interplay of observation and reason within a committed scientific community. This allows agreement amongst many with different backgrounds.

But the non scientist may say that the Christian will believe that ultimately the cow's udder was created by God. Therefore this should be reflected in all that she does. The difficulty of this is that it becomes somewhat impractical. You can imagine a lab report having to be written as, 'The test tube, which is made possible by God creating the chemicals to make the glass, was filled, which was only possible because God in creation enabled men and women to do such things, with water, which was created by God.' Reports and articles would become very long!

The historian John Brooke[37] has pointed out that in the seventeenth century there was a conscious attempt by early members of the Royal Society to drop questions of final causes from their scientific enquiries. These founders of what we call modern science were deeply religious, and believed that God had created all things. However, in order to allow them to pursue their research unhindered by the religious controversies of the day, they developed a method of science which did not have to refer to God as the cause of everything all of the time.

We need to note that this is only justified when confined to the scientific method and does not rule out the Creator God. Christians believe that God is the source of all events, but to specify that in each scientific paper is not necessary. Just because the scientific method is silent about God, it should not be then argued that this disproves God.

2. A recognition of where science has come from

As we have seen science is not a computer program but involves personal judgements. It is because of this that science will involve assumptions including religious beliefs. This was clearly brought home to me while I was working with an Indian physicist. We were considering the question of whether the Universe would expand forever or at some point collapse back onto itself. The observational evidence was at that stage (and still is) somewhat ambiguous but he argued strongly for a collapsing Universe. When I questioned him on why he preferred this model he said that if the Universe collapsed it might 'bounce' into a new Universe, and as a Hindu this fitted with his belief in reincarnation. Now of course he would not let his religious preference become more important than the evidence, but it is a reminder of the way science is more than just method. The historian of science R Hooykaas commented on this:

> 'One cannot dissect one's personality into a scientist, a philosopher, a citizen and a believer. . . . In every age the general intellectual atmosphere is determined by unspoken presuppositions on which all discussion proceeds, and only when these implicit assumptions are no longer shared does it become comparatively easy to recognise them. . . . No discipline, not even natural science, exists without preconceived notions; our science undergoes the influence of our philosophy and both find their roots in metaphysical "religious" preconceptions.'[38]

So then, is there a 'Christian' science? Hooykaas goes on to say that if we look for such a thing 'we should be acting like a man who hunts for his spectacles while they are on his nose. Modern science and technology to a great extent are the fruits of Christianity.'

This statement by a historian of science is based on the importance of the Christian world view for the development of modern science. As we have seen the foundations of science were created by the Greeks who pioneered the use of mathematics and saw science as a rational exercise. However, they saw nature as eternal and uncreated. This coupled to a disregard for manual labour meant neglect of experiment and applied science. I once saw a cartoon of a woman saying to her friend while pointing to her husband asleep on a sofa, 'He's an environmentalist. He won't cut the grass'. Nature was more to be worshipped than actively explored. In addition, they believed that the nature could largely be deduced from logic without the need for observation and experiment. They were 'by reason alone' scientists.

Much of medieval science followed the Greek picture. However, the scientific revolution of the seventeenth century which was really the beginning of what we know as modern science was based on a much different picture. In a series of articles in the journal *Mind* in the 1930s, M B Foster argued that the Christian world view was a major part of this picture.[39] Although historians may disagree on just how influential this Christian world view was, it is clear that science as we know it grew up in a specifically Christian culture whereas in other cultures it did not.

A number of elements were important in the biblical picture which helped this growth:

(a) As the Universe is created by God's free will, you had to observe the Universe to discover its nature. God is not bound to our understanding or logic. This meant that observations were important.

(b) As God is a God of order you would expect to see laws in the Universe. It would not be confusing and irrational.

(c) As humanity is made in the image of God there was the expectation that we could understand that order.

(d) Belief in one God rather than a multitude of gods controlling different parts of nature meant that the Universe was not under different legislation in different places. There should be a consistency of the laws of physics throughout the Universe.

(e) Experiments were right to do as you no longer feared the gods of nature. Indeed, with the Universe being created and put under the dominion of humans, there was a divine mandate to explore. You were not poking your nose into the workings of the gods but exploring what God had given you the capacity to do.

(f) The example of a God who became a human being and worked as a carpenter's son reinforced the idea that technical labour was not inferior.

Of course, the use of reason and mathematics came down from the Greeks and there were other influences in the development of modern science in the seventeenth century. Not least among them was the way the Reformation helped to reject formalised church authority, and gave confidence to explore and ask questions.

Nevertheless, these six foundation stones of modern science owe a great deal to Christianity. Modern science combines both observation of the world with reason. It assumes that the Universe is intelligible to us, that is, there are laws to the Universe and we can understand them. It further assumes that there is a consistency to these laws and it is right to explore the Universe to its fullest extent. In addition, modern science is based on technical labour, whether the construction of a space telescope, or simply washing out the test tubes!

This means for the Christian that the ability to do science is a gift from God in the way that he has created the Universe and ourselves. Of course, those who are not Christians will not be compelled to belief in God because of these considerations. Both Christians and non-Christians share the same scientific method. For Christians, acknowledging the basis of this method will be a source of thankfulness and affirmation. For those who are not Christians, it is worth pondering the question of how science can be done at all. For example, why is the Universe intelligible to us?

3. Unique motive

Science is awe-inspiring and it is intellectually satisfying. It is pursued for these and many other motives. But Christians see their science as 'thinking God's thoughts after him'. This was a major motive in the growth of science. Over the entrance to the Cavendish Laboratory in Cambridge are the words from

Psalm 111:2 'Great are the works of the Lord, they are pondered by all who delight in them.'

In my own life, I became a Christian before going to University to study physics. As my Christian faith grew my interest in science grew. As a small boy, any observers would say I had an unhealthy interest in electricity pylons in Northumberland! The reason for this was that my father was a planning engineer with the electricity board and he was responsible for the pylons. I was interested because of the relationship. That is a small picture of my own growing interest in science. As I was growing in relationship with the God of creation who revealed himself as 'Father', so I was more and more eager to find out more about what he had done.

Dr A Kuyper, founder of the Free (Reformed) University of Amsterdam once wrote, 'There is not an inch of secular life of which Christ does not say, It belongs to me'. The Christian's motive in doing scientific research will not be to become Lord of creation, but to give glory to the One who is truly Lord.

4. Moral dimension

Scientists often view the world as a machine apart from God. This has sometimes led to a feeling that we can use and exploit everything. We are the king of creation. On the other extreme our current ecological crisis has led some to reject science and technology totally, and paved the way theologically to a return to worshipping nature. Nature is not seen as an impersonal machine but rather an organism with all things intricately joined together. This means that we are just the same as the rest of nature, and what right have we to interfere with nature if it is divine?

The biblical view in contrast is not of the world as machine *or* organism but of kingdom under the rule of God. This gives to science a moral dimension. 'The earth is the Lord's and everything in it' (Ps 24:1), so we need to be careful what we do. Science has been given to us by God in creation to use under the mandate of caring for the world and for one another. Thus science may be able to do things, which we may feel as Christians should not be done. The questions that this provokes will be picked up in the next chapter.

What is a scientist . . . according to the Bible

In the light of the above we are now in a position to describe the Christian understanding of what the scientist is and should be:

The scientist as map maker God has given to us the capacity to explore the Universe, to understand its patterns and to record them. We work at constantly improving the map, which involves observing, correcting, and producing models of what is really there. Our maps are descriptions of the order which God both creates and sustains. These maps give us a good picture of the Universe and can also be used for manipulating the world under God's kingdom.

The scientist as commentator The great thing about sports commentators is that they do not just describe the action, they also help to interpret the game to the viewer or listener. These experts give insights which sometimes you would miss without them. These insights give a better understanding of what is going on as well as often provoking a sense of wonder at the subtle skill of the players.

The scientist has responsibility under God to help others understand the amazing Universe which God has created. Such insights will often lead to a sense of awe and wonder. This means that the role of the scientist should include the task of communication. Too often this has been neglected in the training and everyday work of scientists. It is interesting that during the current funding crisis of British science, part of the blame has been directed at the scientists themselves. The public and the politicians have not been engaged in the excitement and achievement of science in a way that would actually help funding. The need is for popular communication. The Christian will feel that this is about telling the works of the Lord.

The scientist as steward Within the world as creation, God appoints us stewards on his behalf. In the first chapter of Genesis, God gives humanity 'dominion' (Gen. 1:26, 28). Some recent writers have attacked this concept. Lyn White wrote that 'Christianity bears a huge burden of guilt' for the ecological problem. But this is to confuse dominion with uncaring domination. Our mandate from God is to work as managers or stewards. Adam and Eve were placed in the garden to tend it. We are given a real role in caring for the available resources on behalf of our boss. He allows the use of resources for our need and gives us the ability to use the plough or the atom. That is, conservation not preservation is the Christian mandate.

James Lovelock, famous for the so-called 'Gaia hypothesis' which describes how the ecosystem of a planet can be viewed as a single system, wrote recently, 'I would sooner expect a goat to succeed as a gardener than expect humans to become stewards of the Earth.'[40] Christians would disagree. Humans are given the responsibility of stewardship although Lovelock is surely right that we have not made a very good job of it.

There is in the concept of stewardship the responsibility to actively do science. As Donald MacKay comments:

> 'In place of the craven fear instilled by a pagan theology of nature – the fear of being regarded as an unwelcome and over-inquisitive intruder in matters that are not his business – the Christian who finds scientific talents in his tool bag has quite a different fear – the fear that his Father should judge him guilty of neglecting his stewardly responsibilities by failing to pursue the opportunities for good that may be opened up by the new developments'[41]

Can the Christian learn science from non-Christians?

If we acknowledge that science is a gift of God in creation, then we must accept that this gift is for everyone, both Christians and those who are not. I remember being approached after a talk by a young man who was getting into terrible difficulty with his University department. He was a fine young Christian but believed that you had to be a Christian in order to do science properly. He felt that his views on geology and biology disagreed with those of his lecturers because they were not Christians, and therefore inferior scientists.

The mistake he was making was a failure to recognise that God has given science as a gift in creation. Now of course, science can be used to argue against God, but as we saw above, this is scientism not science. The scientist who is not a Christian may not share the same motivation or moral dimension to science, but is able to be a good map maker because of God's gift. The great Reformation theologian John Calvin[42] pointed out that if we reject other learning, then we offend the Holy Spirit who has bestowed such gifts on all.

The Bible itself is very clear that God speaks 'in various ways' (Heb. 1:1). Part of his speaking is in the glories of creation (see Ps 19:1, Rom 1:18-20). While acknowledging that human minds cannot discern how we can be reconciled to God, nevertheless we are not left completely in the dark. It is this understanding that encourages some Christians to speak of 'natural theology', that is discerning something of God from his works of creation. Such an approach was followed up to a point in the previous chapter where there seemed to be pointers from the natural world to God. The fascinating thing was that such pointers were often acknowledged by both Christians and non-Christians alike.

How different is science from theology?

Some will say this is all very well, understanding science. But where does theology fit in? Are not the two just totally different? Richard Dawkins states that in contrast to science, 'Faith is the great cop-out, the great excuse to evade the need to think and evaluate evidence.'[43] The trouble is, statements like that themselves are a cop-out from fully understanding the nature of Christian belief. If you think about the nature of the theology, you begin to see that there are both similarities and differences with science.

A lab coat that merges into a dog collar!

It will be surprising to many that there are actually quite a few similarities between theology and science. In all of this I assume that theology has a 'critical realist' view of the world. That is, there something objective out there which is to be explored with the recognition that our ways of talking and understanding never give us the whole picture.

Of course, just as in science there are different views on this. The Cambridge theologian Don Cupitt and his 'Sea of Faith' network follow a form of theological idealism. God is not the objective reality at the centre of theology's exploration. God is only really there in the mind, a human construction to help us cope with the world. This is not the place for a detailed defence against such a position. It has been given elsewhere.[44] It is sufficient to note here that much that was said against scientific idealism can be said against theological idealism.

So what are the similarities?

Christian belief does not proceed by reason alone. God cannot be proved or his nature figured out by logic and the back of an envelope (or hymn book!). Reason has always been an important aspect of the Christian understanding of God, but it is not the only aspect. Can God create a stone heavier than he can lift? This may be a question of interest around the philosophy department seminar room, but actually does not get us that far in our understanding.

There have been many attempted proofs of the existence of God such as:

- the Universe looks to be designed therefore there must be a designer – God
- the Universe needs a cause for its existence therefore that must be God

- the most perfect being would be not perfect if he did not exist, therefore God must exist

These arguments however have all fallen foul to counter arguments. Logic eventually runs out, which is not terribly surprising when one is dealing with a God who is greater than our Universe.

Christian belief has an important place for data or evidence. Christian theology deals with what is given. This includes of course religious experience. The Alistair Hardy Research Centre, founded by a biologist, has collected data on religious experience over many years. The results are that over 60% of people have experiences which point to there being more to the Universe that meets the eye. These experiences include a sense of the unity of all things, awe and reverence, joy, guilt, forgiveness and peace. Theology takes seriously this aspect of people's experience in the world as an indication of the way God relates to his creation.

However, it would be a wrong impression to believe that Christianity has only the data of individual personal experience. Central to its claims for truth is the witness of history. That is, the Christian claim is that our knowledge of God comes from what the philosopher Francis Schaeffer called 'brute facts'. They are brute facts because God's revelation of himself in Christ took place at a point in the space-time history of the Universe. These are public facts which can be examined and debated by everyone rather than just personal religious experiences. The basis of Christianity is a set of events which occurred in history, especially the events surrounding the life, death and resurrection of Jesus of Nazareth.

In fact, the word 'gospel' as well as meaning good news can also mean epoch-making event. Those events became of prime importance to the Christian community and great care was taken in writing them down.

For example, Luke at the beginning of his Gospel states:

'Many have undertaken to draw up an account of the things that have been fulfilled among us, just as they were handed down to us by those who from the first were eye-witnesses and servants of the word. Therefore, since I myself have carefully investigated everything from the beginning, it seemed good also to me to write an orderly account for you, most excellent Theophilus, so that you may know the certainty of the things you have been taught' (Lk 1:1–4)

We do not know who Theophilus was, but it is clear that Luke was writing a carefully researched account of the events. Now these events in themselves do not compel belief, but they are there to be assessed. Just as the good scientist will weigh the evidence and make a judgement upon it, the case for Christianity is in some ways similar.

I was once in conversation with a physics undergraduate, who in a rather aggressive way was criticising me for having Christian faith while being a scientist. The conversation went something like this:

'David, as a scientist you should not have faith but trust the evidence!'

'Have you ever examined the reliability of the New Testament documents?'

'No, but I did RE at school.'

'Have you ever looked at the historical evidence for Jesus?'

'No, but I saw a programme on Channel 4 which said that he might not exist.'

'Have you looked at the historical evidence for the resurrection of Jesus, the empty tomb, the appearances and the growth of the Christian church?'

'Not really, but it wouldn't make much difference because I know the dead don't rise.'

'Have you ever considered the full implications of the Christian message for understanding individuals, society and the world?'

'Of course not, I haven't the time.'

'Who then has the faith? Your statements are based on such

flimsy premises that if you were to do the same in science you wouldn't even make it to the second year never mind earn your degree.'

I think I was a little hard on the young man, but so much scepticism of Christianity is based on the belief that Christians have no evidence. Christians have no proof, but they do have evidence.

Christian belief involves an interplay of experience and interpretation. These events or 'brute facts' need interpretation. At the end of John's account of Jesus he writes this:

> 'Jesus did many other miraculous signs in the presence of his disciples, which are not recorded in this book. But these are written that you may believe that Jesus is the Christ, the Son of God, and that by believing you may have life in his name' (Jn 20:30).

Events by themselves do not make up a gospel. John in his account is giving the reason behind the events, that is that Jesus came to give new life to those who trust in him. To take another example, the death of Jesus is a historical event. But its significance for Christians is what it means, in terms of God's love, forgiveness and a new start.

The role of the community is important in testing truth claims. In Paul's first letter to the Christians at Corinth, he deals with what is true and false doctrine in the early church. He stresses his own authority as an Apostle (1 Cor 4:1), the tradition that he has received (1 Cor 11:23) and the importance of the body of believers to test claims. In particular, when dealing with those in the church who were prophesying he asked that what was said should be weighed carefully by the community (1 Cor 14:29). From the Council of Jerusalem (Acts 15) throughout the history of the church, the community has been important in deciding truth or falsehood. The community of the world-wide church although not as close as the scientific community, shares a common language, experience and tradition.

Other similarities can be drawn. For example, some have argued that truth within theology is judged on similar criteria to scientific theories.

Where the dog collar and lab coat do not fit

Having said all of the above we need to recognise some important differences between science and theology.

There is a different degree of personal involvement. Science for all of the personal judgements involved minimises the personal as much as possible. We learn that at school, when scientific reports do not begin with 'I put the chemical into the test-tube', but with 'The chemical was placed in the test-tube'. Now as we have seen this may be a slightly misleading view of science, but for biblical Christianity the personal is never minimised. For all the weighing of evidence, the invitation of the Bible is to participate in a personal relationship, part of which requires risk and trust.

Jesus states this plainly, 'If you hold to my teaching, you are really my disciples. Then you will know the truth and the truth will set you free' (Jn 8:31). To know the truth in biblical terms depends on personal involvement. This should not surprise us once we recognise that the object of our exploration is not just an impersonal physical reality but a personal God. The former Bishop of Durham, David Jenkins, said, 'God is no object of critical investigation, he is the subject of faith and hope, of obedience, of love, of longing'.

I might ask, 'Does my wife love me?' Now there could be hard evidence to help me in the answer. If she always screamed and ran away when she saw me, that might point to a certain conclusion! But in the end, I would only know by becoming involved in the relationship. To do that requires trusting what she says, and the risk of trusting my very self in her hands. No amount of evidence can take away the degree of personal involvement needed to know.

A recent book was entitled *To Know as We are Known*[45]. In many ways this reflects the biblical teaching. To know God we need both to actively explore and to have an openness to receive from him (1 Jn 4:19).

In fact, it has been argued that the physical sciences, the social sciences such as psychology and sociology, and theology share many similarities in exploring the world but have a different degrees of personal involvement.

Science and theology ask different types of question of the world. Critics like Dawkins see both science and Christian belief in competition, giving competing explanations for the same phenomenon such as the origin of the Universe. At a most basic level, people have differentiated science and religion by saying that science answers 'how' questions, while religion answers 'why' questions. Now although this is oversimplified, it does remind us that they do look at the world with different questions, some of which may be separate, some of which may overlap.

A couple of years ago I was invited to the Greenbelt arts festival to debate science and religion with Dr Peter Atkins. Dr Atkins is a research chemist at Oxford and a good populariser of science. He also happens to be a very aggressive atheist, incidentally one of the few who will actually stand up for what he believes. As we debated with the audience it became clear that on the scientific issues he and I had much in common. Our main disagreement was over whether once you had a scientific explanation of an event, that was sufficient. He argued that it was.

However, the important thing to remember is that there can be different but compatible explanations for an event. An old illustration is to ask why is the kettle boiling? One answer is to say that energy is being given to the water molecules until bubbles form. Another answer is to say that we want a cup of tea. Both are valid but different, and in fact both are needed for a full understanding of why the kettle is boiling.

This may sound simple enough but it is often very difficult for people to hold to in practice. Michael Poole suggests that the common tendency to think that one type of explanation can oust another of a different type is rather like one noisy fledgling in a nest trying to evict the others. We may get mentally frustrated by things we cannot explain and so any type of explanation relieves this frustration so that other types are not sought or even denied.[46]

So, although it may be attractive to say the Universe came from a Big Bang and that does away with God, such a statement misunderstands science and theology. We shall explore this further in Chapter Five.

There is no parallel in science to Christianity's claim of historical revelation. The Bible is a book which from beginning to end insists that God is not there primarily to be explored, but to be listened to (Dt 29:29). Human beings, because of our limited minds and rebellion which has cut us from the life of God, cannot of ourselves find God. But in his love for us, God finds us, revealing truth to us. God does not reveal everything, but he does reveal some things. Christians from many different theological traditions have centred the authority of this revelation on the Bible. This is quite different from science.

Thus truth claims within Christian belief are not just decided by the community, but there will always be reference back to the Bible. This is not just holding on to dogmatic traditionalism, it is the belief that God has spoken and continues to speak in an authoritative way through the pages of the Bible.

Conflict or fruitful interaction?

So to return again to the first question, how do we know what we think we know in theology? I suggest it is the 'subtle interplay of experience and interpretation involving personal judgements within a committed community exploring an objective personal reality'. If you compare this definition with the definition of science you will see the similarity. The methods of science and theology are not totally different once you delve beneath the popular caricatures. Science is not done by computers and does not lead to proof. Christian belief is not 'throw your brain away' dogma and is based on evidence. The important difference is that theology explores a personal reality who has revealed himself to us.

Why if this is the case, you might ask, is the popular stereotype of science in conflict with religion around? Many people see the conflict of science and religion to have had a long history, and coming about for purely intellectual motives. In fact, although much of this conflict was focused at the time of Darwin, it was T H Huxley and others who set out on purpose to build a 'conflict' view. Huxley was known as 'Darwin's bulldog', but his main purpose was to free professional science from the influence and control of the church. By seeing science and religion as totally opposed this helped the process. Huxley organised a scientific religion, with such things as scientific sermons and 'Sunday evenings for the people'.

As science developed its own independence, Christians often criticised science, frightened by its success. Christians need to recognise that they have been guilty in the last century of neglecting the biblical basis of science and not affirming those Christians who are scientists. The Christian church has often taken on board the popular stereotypes of conflict, feeling that it has to attack science on its own ground.

Yet in all of this there have been many scientists who have with integrity held together their science and their Christian belief. We will examine this more fully in Chapter Seven. But if both science and religion are exploring the objective reality of a God created Universe, we should expect in John Polkinghorne's phrase 'fruitful interaction'. We should also expect to find issues where both have something to say, and the question is then, are we prepared to listen to both?

How do we boldly go?

In the light of all of this, perhaps we need to be reminded of two things as we attempt to explore the world. The first is the importance of humility. T H Huxley said that we have to sit down before the facts like a little child. We need to be open to the evidence that God gives us and not trust our own theories too much. His thoughts are greater than our thoughts and the creature cannot reasonably expect to be like God in all knowledge. There are always going to be aspects of God and the Universe which lie beyond us. This is not to justify our laziness by an appeal to mystery, it is simply a recognition that we are finite and fallen creatures.

However, secondly, as God is the self revealing God we go forward in hope. We do not have to wrestle secrets from nature, fighting against mysterious and jealous gods. Human beings are invited and equipped to inquire by a God who is not mean with the truth.

4

Has Science All the Moral Answers?
(Rob Frost)

Contemporary scientific research appears to be throwing up more questions than answers. These questions are often extremely complex, and those who think that science ethics are as clear as black and white are naive in the extreme. Science does not have all the answers, and there is an urgent need for Christians to get involved in the delicate ethical issues of scientific research.

Living the truth!

I walked across the small veranda and pushed the front door slightly, it creaked open, and I stepped inside. The old wooden house was very silent as I walked slowly from room to room with everything just as it had been, all those years before. I was in downtown Atlanta, Georgia, in the boyhood home of the Reverend Doctor Martin Luther King, the Baptist minister who advocated non-violence in the black civil rights struggle in the United States. He was assassinated in 1968.

This was the house where he grew up, and the home in which many of his ideas were formed. There was his baseball bat, his Monopoly board laid out for a game, and his school books, strewn across the table as if he'd left his homework, half finished. I stood and looked out of the window on the poor downtown neighbourhood, and wondered again at the impact which this one short life had made upon the world.

Down the street a few yards, beside the Luther King Memorial Sculpture, was a museum and audio-visual theatre which told the story of King's fight for black human rights in America. I found it all fascinating because when I was a teenager his life and his death made a dramatic impact on me.

I think it was the sermon notes which, of all the exhibits, intrigued me most. There they were, written out laboriously word for word with each phrase weighed and checked and each page filled with scribbling. All over the script there were crossed-out words and minor additions or subtractions to the flow of the text. He must have gone over his sermons time and time again before he was satisfied with the rhythm and the style. Sermons which, even to this day, echo round the world with the resonance of his delivery.

King was a Christian who took the social implications of the gospel seriously. It wasn't enough just to believe, for he recognised, as James did, that 'faith without works is dead'. One of King's sermons called *A knock at midnight* has always intrigued me, for it is as relevant today as the day he preached it. Especially so, perhaps, to those who serve in the front line of scientific research.

'It is midnight within the moral order,' King declared. 'At midnight colours lose their distinctiveness and become a sullen shade of grey. Moral principles have lost their distinctiveness . . . absolute right and absolute wrong are a matter of what the majority is doing. Right and wrong are relative to the likes and dislikes and the customs of a particular community.'

Yet, despite this 'moral midnight' in which King lived, worked, and died, he lived a life which impacted the whole world. Though the situation was difficult, he did not remain silent. Though the bright colours of justice and equality had lost their distinctiveness, his life shone with righteous anger. He was scorned and ridiculed, yet his witness cast a bright light on to the dark night of urban racism.

For those Christians who are involved in contemporary

science there are new battles to be fought. The days are gone when the decisions as to what is 'right' and what is 'wrong' can be judged by a lone researcher working in isolation. The modern scientist often has to work as a member of a team where 'moral principles have lost their distinctiveness'. Their judgements may well be contested by the majority and they may be overruled by those whose ethical preferences are strikingly different.

No matter how difficult it may seem, such Christians are called to walk the lonely road which King walked. They may have to bear their witness to Christian moral absolutes even when they feel completely isolated. The cost may be high and might involve withdrawing from a programme, foregoing promotion, or even losing a job. There are times in scientific research when Christians will have to take a stand, no matter how painful it might be.

The moral maze

Whenever overseas guests are staying with me, I try to take them to Hampton Court, the beautiful old Palace beside the River Thames. One of my favourite spots in the Palace garden is a park bench just outside the Maze. The view from this bench provides a cheap afternoon's entertainment! Look at the turnstile and see the crowds of tourists entering the Maze, happy and confident, and assured that a few old British hedges won't defeat them! Then, turn and look at the well-camouflaged exit. See them coming out again, stressed and dishevelled, having walked in ever-decreasing circles for up to an hour! What may seem simple to the outsider can feel very complicated once you're within!

I sometimes shudder when I hear Christians making definitive statements about moral and ethical science issues, but whose views seem more based on prejudice than on understanding. Like the Hampton Court experience, the 'moral maze' often looks simpler from the outside than within!

Science has thrown up a diverse range of new ethical problems in recent years. New powers always create difficult ethical problems because there are no precedents on which to build new guidelines. New technological power brings positive and negative forces into society. Take almost any area of modern scientific advance and you are faced with a complex agenda of ethical and moral issues. Here, then, are few examples of life in the modern maze!

The nuclear issue

One might assume that this was a simple example of science gone mad! A uranium nucleus was first split successfully in 1938. Three years later, in 1941, the Americans learnt that the top physicists left in Nazi Germany were busy constructing a nuclear bomb.

This left the Allies in a moral maze! Should they wait for that to happen, and so allow Hitler to attain world domination, or should they to try to get there first? Einstein and others tried to persuade President Roosevelt to give the go-ahead for a project to create the bomb. It led to the greatest organised effort of physicists and chemists in history.

It was a straight choice between evil, and greater evil. Grey and grey?

The ecological issue

The invention of the internal combustion engine led to the development of the motor car. It could be argued that this has increased the quality of life of countless millions of working people and enabled them to travel conveniently and cheaply. It has brought pleasure, mobility, and an economic form of transport to generations of families.

At the same time, however, it could be demonstrated that this one technological advance has caused huge environmental damage. There are currently over twenty-six million vehicles in the UK alone, and the Department of Transport estimates that traffic on our roads could double by the year 2025. Motor vehicles are the fastest-growing source of air pollution in the UK today, pumping out a cocktail of health-threatening pollutants.

Has this technological advance done more good than harm, or harm than good? Grey and grey?

The energy issue

Nuclear energy has promised cheap power. Compared to the human cost of coalmining, or the world's diminishing resources of fuel oil, it would appear to provide the perfect solution to the world's ever-growing demand for energy. Anyone who has ever taken the luxury coach tour around Sellafield in Cumbria cannot fail to be impressed by the care which those involved in the production of nuclear power seem to take to ensure safety.

Yet many would claim that this development has cast a dark shadow over the world. It has produced a threat which became a dark reality one day in a small Russian town called Chernobyl. Certainly, the heart-rending images of Chernobyl's diseased children cannot but make us wonder at what has been unleashed on the world. Should cheap energy have ever cost the world so dearly?

Images of miners with lung disease or of Chernobyl's children in the cancer ward. Grey and grey?

The medical issue

Widespread interest in the problems of bioethics dates from the 1960's and 1970's. At about this time developments like heart transplantation and the allocation of scarce life-saving resources such as dialysis machines raised serious questions about the prioritising of patients for limited resources.

The preservation of life for a doubtful long-term outcome can pose insoluble ethical problems. I remember sitting in a small doctor's office in a South London hospital and discussing the pros and cons of continuing a patient's treatment or of turning off a life support system. Suddenly, the decisions were not theoretical, but the awesome responsibility of deciding whether the patient would be dead by two o'clock that afternoon. Advancement of medical science can produce outcomes which the patient himself would never have wanted.

Whose life is it anyway? Grey and grey?

The euthanasia issue

Those involved in various branches of medical research and who are health professionals may be faced with decisions which are popularly labelled 'euthanasia'. Most Christians would recognise that we are stewards of God with respect to life. We are answerable and accountable to God for life itself and how we use it. We are not free to return that loan whenever we feel like it.

Yet, even here, there are Christians who disagree. From personal experience I have to admit that, when I was faced with a terminally ill patient suffering unbearable agony of mind and body, that the arguments for continuation of treatment sounded very hollow. Days of acute human suffering can seem as dark as the midnight hour.

Decisions between prolonging life and ending life can be agonising in the extreme. Grey and grey?

The life issue

In a detailed review of the current abortion debate John Stott expounded Psalm 139 in detail in his book *Issues Facing Christians Today*. He concluded: 'The foetus is neither a growth in the mother's body, nor even a potential human being, but already a human life who, though not yet mature, has the potentiality of growing into the fullness of the individual humanity he already possesses.'[47]

Yet while most Christians concur with John Stott's findings, situations do exist such as the endangerment of a mother's health or the termination of a foetus resulting from rape where even the ardent 'pro-lifer' can hesitate. Those who are looking to Christian ethics to always give a simplistic 'yes' or 'no' answer may sometimes be disappointed.

Anyone who has agonised with a childless couple over the ethical rights and wrongs of invitro-fertilisation will know that the issues are not always as clear as we'd like them to be. Some view this process as a blasphemy against God's natural way of giving life. Others argue that if the church teaches that procreation and child-rearing are part of true family life, how can it forbid the provision of such children when natural fertilisation seems impossible? Joyous pictures of families with IVF children can look very convincing. In the disputed territory between unnatural means of fertilisation and unnatural means of termination there lies an ethical minefield!

The rights of parents to have children, the rights of a woman over her own body, and the rights of a foetus to fulfil its existing and future human potential. Grey and grey?

The human embryo issue

The ethics of research on human embryos and the possibilities of genetic manipulation might seem to be straightforward. Any hint of wholesale genetic engineering of human traits in the name of perfectionism is considered unbiblical by many Christians. Creation is complete, and the Genesis texts which point to this are drawn upon to support the argument. If genetic experimentation continues a future full of danger is prophesied.

Yet even the Warnock Report, with its fairly clear-cut recommendations on many issues such as surrogacy and IVF had to admit in its section on embryo research that: 'Although the questions of when life or personhood begin appear to be questions of fact susceptible to straightforward answers, we hold that the answers to such questions in fact are complex amalgams of factual and moral arguments.'

It is clear that even those who have devoted hundreds of hours of committee time to exploring such subjects do not find the answers simple! Some would argue that embryo research provides important data for the advance of humanity, and that such research can be a means of eradicating many genetic problems which cause untold misery. Ruth Chadwick observed:

'It is argued by those who have an interest in genetics that by continuing to produce babies with genetic defects, we are adding to the 'genetic load' that is carried by the species. By not exercising quality control over the species now, we are not only bringing into the world individuals who have a low probability of a satisfying quality of life, but we are also storing up trouble for future generations, who will be faced with the results of our lack of forethought.'[48]

Genetic experimentation, the road to health or the road to hell? Grey and grey?

Simplistic solutions?

I wish that I could specify neat, cut and dried ethical solutions for each issue raised above! I would like to lay down a clear and simple set of 'guidelines' which could be applied to each of the scenarios described. Some Christians feel able to lay down such ground-rules, but I'm afraid that I must remain sceptical.

Don't get me wrong! I am convinced that there is right and wrong. There is 'within God's will' and 'outside God's will'. But we can only determine what falls into each category as we scrutinise each stage of a project's development as it happens, every new ethical dilemma as we approach it, and every decision as it is being made.

This may appear 'the easy option', but in fact I believe it is the more difficult way. Those who can judge everything by clearly defined and immovable parameters are to be envied. It is much more difficult to identify the forces of good and evil in the flux of an ever-changing ethical dynamic.

Christians working in such fields need all the help they can get in sifting through the complicated philosophical, ethical and religious questions. Simplistic solutions, then, are not appropriate. John Stott wrote:

'Neat, cut and dried solutions are usually impossible. Simplistic short-cuts which ignore the real issues, are unhelpful. At the same time, it is not Christian to give up in despair . . . he has given us the Bible and its witness to Christ, in order to direct and control our thinking . . . as we absorb its teaching, our thoughts will increasingly conform to his.'[49]

I am sceptical when people compose pithy slogans which claim to give Christian 'views' on subjects which are often very complex and difficult for the layman to understand. I believe that the church needs scientists who will take theology and Christian ethics seriously, and who will seek the mind of Christ in areas of debate from which many of us are precluded by our lack of knowledge and understanding.

Christians involved in science should never underestimate the complexity of the moral task in which they are involved! They may find themselves contributing to scientific knowledge which will be used for purposes they would oppose. They may have to make decisions which are not at all clear-cut and find themselves in the seemingly incomprehensible world of the moral maze! Professor A van den Beukel, of the University of Delft in the Netherlands observed:

'The work of scientists has unmistakable social consequences, positive and negative. In by far the great majority of instances these consequences are outside their reach. They cannot be foreseen, and if they could be foreseen they could not be weighed. Once they happen they cannot be undone.'[50]

In conversation with scientists from different backgrounds I hear how difficult it is to be sensitive to ethical questions when the pressure for results is on. It is not easy, they tell me, to appeal to Christian distinctives when their colleagues claim equal validity for their viewpoints. Some researchers work as members of teams where different ethical perspectives are constantly vying for control. One scientist sounded genuinely concerned as she told me:

'In my department . . . speed is of the essence. When I first started we ran tests in order, and weighed each result before proceeding to the next stage. Now, the tests run concurrently. The pressure is on. There is only one question ... how long until launch? There is little time for ethical niceties when the over-riding priority is cost-effectiveness!'

Sometimes the Christian research scientist may struggle with issues which are not at all clear-cut. Even different Christians may disagree about how to decide them! Sometimes there is no 'proof-text' on hand to support one thesis against another. The decisions don't appear to be a question of 'black' against 'white' but of 'grey against grey'! One research worker for a large pharmaceutical company confided that:

'Today, the whole process is market-driven. The questions are not so much about which drug may do the most good, but which drug is likely to claim the best market advantage.'

New scientific discoveries may lead to a chain of development over which participating scientists have little or no control. Their contribution to a project may eventually be used for purposes with which they would fundamentally disagree. As one post-doctoral researcher told me:

'It is sometimes impossible for me to envisage how my work will be used. How am I to know if my research for the development of stronger stainless steel sinks for the third world may be used by someone else to develop a new form of shrapnel for armaments!'

No one should underestimate the ethical dilemmas which have to be faced when we work in science. But this is where Christ calls his followers to be, living in the real world. The Christian involved in science may often find himself looking for a way out of the moral maze.

Where do we begin?

However, if Jesus is incarnate in the world, then he is with us in the moral maze. He is immersed in these complex moral decisions and he can lead us through these moral dilemmas. His teaching is relevant, and he can help us to apply the unchanging values of the Christian gospel to the issues which confront us.

Christopher Merchant, an environmental physicist with a belief in the absolute, argues that there are such solid terms of reference applicable to all cultures. Applying Einstein's principle of relativity to the moral chaos pervading society, he wrote:

> '. . . good behaviour is a cultural invariant . . . "Love your neighbour as yourself" (Matthew 22:39) is my candidate for a culturally invariant principle. As you can see from the reference, it isn't a new idea – others have formulated similar laws, and even Jesus was quoting a much older source. As a principle, it is easy to learn, and the practice of it lasts a lifetime.'[51]

Even in the confusion of the 'moral maze', therefore, there are 'invariants' which we must hold on to at the heart of our faith. We must listen for the voice of conscience so that we know when to say 'Enough is enough. So far, but no further!'

Even in the grey tones of midnight, God wants to guide us into uses of science which are constructive and life-enhancing. He wants us to use scientific processes in partnership with him. He wants us to share in the redemption, healing and salvation of a broken world.

We need to know the moral invariants for each context. We must identify the standards which are non-negotiable. We must recognise the boundaries which must be drawn, the lines laid down, and the barriers which need to be erected to prevent us straying from 'right' to 'wrong' or from 'good' to 'evil'.

There are times when we are called to shine the light of the gospel onto the grey areas of contemporary science. We must recognise when the practice of contemporary science travels contrary to the practice of contemporary faith. We must be willing to stand up and be counted. Father John Mahoney,

Professor of Moral and Social Theology at King's College, London observed that:

> 'For the believer, one such sacrifice which cannot be made in favour of any other consideration is that of his belief, not simply in the sense of abandoning religious belief, but of so compartmentalising it in his mind as to render it atrophied and ineffective, even when accompanied by such religious performances as worship and church attendance.' [52]

As Mahoney says, our faith is more than singing hymns and saying prayers. It impinges on every aspect of our work as scientists. Christian faith is not something which is separate from the rest of life. We must allow science to affect faith, and faith to influence science.

No matter how minor our role in a scientific project, we bear our share of the moral responsibility. If we feel that we're in a 'moral maze' we must pray for spiritual and intellectual sensitivity to find the way out. If this sensitivity becomes blunted, we are ineffective as Christians.

We must ask the right questions, examine the ethical standards, speak up for the truth, or we come under judgement for denying Christ in the world. God may forgive us, but will we ever be able to forgive ourselves? In a moving confession Professor van den Beukel had to admit:

> 'In my young years my colleagues and I took the possible social consequences of our work lightly. I don't want to make this mistake again in my old age . . . science has detached human beings and their world from God and even has taken God's place'.[53]

Welcome, then, to the 'moral maze'. The place of contemporary confusion where we struggle to know the mind of Christ in dilemmas beyond our understanding! The place where, when we can't differentiate 'grey' from 'grey' in the darkness of midnight, we pause to listen for his voice. The dark place of shadows called Gethsemane, where we pray with Jesus. . . . 'Not my will, but thine be done.'

Developing a Christian mind

Recently, I was a guest in one of the most peculiar hotels I have ever stayed in. It was a 'hotel training school' situated in Herzliya, just outside Tel Aviv, and it was open to the public.

The army of young Jewish waiters (at times, six per table!) who served us were evidently the fresh intake at the start of a new term. They spilled soup, they dropped potato, they collided with one another in their haste, and their tutor seemed particularly stressed.

'We have tonight, sir, our special . . . Goose Foot. You like?' smiled the young man. I grinned sympathetically. . . 'Yes . . . fine. . . .' I replied. I was somewhat relieved to see that when the dish arrived it was Turkey Breast. Evidently, something had been lost in translation or gained in the haute cuisine!

As I watched the class develop during the week, and saw them progress from a simple buffet to their first clumsy attempts at silver service, one thing became clear. The tutor was attempting to develop within each of them a mind alert to the needs of each guest. As they grew in confidence they began to notice when each water jug needed filling, when the plates were ready to be cleared, or when a guest was trying to catch their eye. They were developing a waiter's mind.

My brother-in-law, who runs fine restaurants, has developed this skill to a fine art. I have watched him standing silently and surveying sixty dinner guests, all at different stages of a five-course meal, and read each table like a book. The waiters scurry from place to place at the slightest nod of his head or movement of his eye.

Take almost any discipline and you will find the application of a trained mind. Take any building, for example, and a developer will see money, an architect potential, an artist perspective, a policeman security, a surveyor safety, a postman postcodes, and a civil servant tax revenue. The trained mind sees things which the rest of us tend to miss!

Harry Blamires, in his book *The Christian Mind* popularised the concept of an intellectual approach to life which is truly Christian. He defined it as 'a mind trained, informed, equipped to handle data of secular controversy within a framework of reference which is constructed of Christian pre-suppositions.'[54].

The Christian who is so equipped will, according to Blamires, 'challenge current prejudices . . . disturb the complacent . . . obstruct the busy pragmatists . . . and question the very foundations of all about him... he is a nuisance!'

The Christian in science needs to look at his subject with a trained mind! He needs to develop a sensitivity to bigger issues than chemical formulae, mathematical equations or computerised test results. The Christian mind must view each stage of scientific development and ask how it fits into God's work of creation and redemption. It seeks out the disputed shades of grey in order to discover a truly Christian ethic for them.

The greatest resource for this work is the Bible, which for the Christian has a greater authority that any other book. It's an authority which rests in the belief that it is God-inspired and not man made. The theologian and philosopher, David Cook observed that:

> 'The Christian believes that Scripture has something to say to the world and to mankind and that something carries authority. However, Biblical authority does not rest in the pages of the Bible itself. This is no paper-pope. Biblical authority stems from its relationship with God.'[55]

The Bible should not be used as a list of 'proof-texts' which can be plucked out to condone or condemn any scientific development. Those who use it as such do God's word a great disservice; for they rip phrases and statements out of context and use God's word without beginning to understand it.

I would advocate a broader view of the Bible which helps us to comprehend the four great dramas in God's story. For each one of them has a different bearing on the world of science ethics:

- The Creation story teaches God's creative activity and the God-likeness of humanity, whose highest fulfilment is to be found in obeying, knowing and worshipping the Creator. There is a lot about 'ownership' and 'steward-ship' here, as we saw in the previous chapter, which is very relevant to ethical discussion.

- The Fall resulted from man's disobedience, and all human alienation, disorientation, and meaninglessness have stemmed from this. Any attempt to discuss ethical state-ments needs to be done against this backdrop for we live in a fallen world, and the forces at work in it are often destructive and inhuman.

- Redemption is God's opportunity to make things new. It began with a covenant with Abraham and looked forward to the coming Messiah. Jesus opened the way for individ-uals to be redeemed and incorporated into a new commu-nity. All those who live and work in partnership with Christ are involved in his redemptive purposes for the world by making the world a more humane and better place.

- The final chapter will be the Consummation of all things when Christ appears again and all pain, decay, sin, sorrow and death will disappear for ever. Christians are not working towards an unknown future, and no matter how hopeless things may seem, the last page of history lies in the ultimate purposes of God.

John Stott urges that the Christian mind should be immersed in these four great epochs of the Biblical story, each one of which gives important ethical insights into the will of God. He wrote:

'This fourfold biblical reality enables Christians to survey the historical landscape within its proper horizons. It sup-plies the true perspective from which to view the unfolding process between two eternities, the vision of God working out his purpose. It gives us a framework in which to fit every-thing, a way of integrating our understanding, the possibility of thinking straight, even about the most complex issues.'[56]

Building on the Bible

We must saturate ourselves in the whole of the Bible's unfolding revelation, not just in the bits which make for good ethical ammunition! Genesis and Exodus, for example, introduce us to important 'value judgements' which appear again and again in God's dealings with his people.

It is clear from the stories of Abraham that God's offer of a covenant relationship means that man is seen is a partner with God. Service to mankind and the world are pinpointed as a vital part of true service to God.

The Wisdom Literature (Proverbs, Job, Ecclesiastes, and the Song of Solomon) gives very practical and relevant teaching. The Prophets took up the great themes of the ten commandments and applied them to their own society and situation.

Amos (760 BC) condemned injustice and the immoral drives of materialism, power and worldly pleasure. Hosea (745 BC) urged the people to love, for God considered that a more important offering of worship than sacrifice. Isaiah (740 BC) urged the people to be loyal to God by lives of 'justice and righteousness'. Micah asked 'what does the Lord require of you but to do justice, and to love kindness, and to walk humbly before your God?' Similar sentiments were preached by Zephaniah, Ezekiel, Zechariah and Malachi.

The gospels tell us about the true humanity which God wants us to live. Christ's teaching in passages like the Beatitudes proclaim some of the basic standards of our civilisation. The humanising effect of the life of Jesus marks him out as someone apart. William Lecky wrote that 'those three short years of active life have done more to regenerate and soften mankind than all the disquisitions of philosophers and the exhortations of moralists.'

John Haught, Professor of Theology at Georgetown University, identifies the transforming effect of Jesus upon others in these words.

'The figure of Jesus the Christ, as it is portrayed in the gospels and as it is imitated and reembodied in contemporary lives, has drawn numerous people into a circle of restored trust and hope. It has done so, I suspect, because it is a representation of universal beauty. . . .'[57]

The Apostle Paul applied Christ's teaching to his own situation, and whilst he was not writing a systematic guide to ethics we can detect many ethical principles in his struggle to discover the will of God for his situation. Paul's ethical emphasis catered for the whole person. He told us to imitate God, Christ and even his own life if we are to live ethical lives. This was not a theory, but something which Paul hammered out on the anvil of his own painful experiences. The Pastoral Epistles were also written with specific situations in mind and contain a rich seam of moral and ethical teaching for those taking the time to unpack it.

Among the many different ways of using the Bible in ethics I would advocate that it should be used as a whole entity. It is the Christian's responsibility to search the Bible and to weigh each part with the rest. It is too easy to pull out simplistic proof texts rather than hearing what God is saying through the whole story.

We must balance verse with verse, book with book and truth with truth. As we are immersed in the four great eras of his dealings with humanity we will begin to develop a 'Christian mind' and to discover his will for the world and his great hope for civilisation. John Stott observed that God:

> '. . . has given us the Bible and its witness to Christ, in order to direct and control our thinking. As we absorb its teaching, our thoughts will increasingly conform to his. This is not because we memorise a lot of proof texts, which we trot out at appropriate moments, each text labelled to answer its own question. It is rather that we have grasped the great themes and principles of Scripture.'[58]

A renewing relationship

A thorough understanding of the Bible is vital to the development of a 'Christian mind', but it is not enough by itself. The scientist who wishes to chart his way through the moral maze also needs a living relationship with Christ which is founded on the creed 'Jesus is Lord'. It's this encounter with the living God which makes his faith powerful and active. The risen Christ is the mainspring for his action. John Polkinghorne observed:

> 'From the earliest times there has been this testimony to encounter with a particular and unique saving action of God in Christ. Its understanding will be no easy matter, but it is common experience, in science as well as religion, that reality is subtle beyond our powers of prior expectation.'[59]

Jesus exerts a living influence on his followers today, not just through his teaching, but through the mystery of Christian conversion and our living relationship with him. Countless Christians claim that Jesus has so affected their lives that he has actually transformed them. Celia Haddon, for instance, the editor of *The Sunday Times Book of Body Maintenance*, stated. 'I needed, desperately needed, some help and comfort in my attempt to lead a good life. Christ offered me that support.'

When a scientist becomes a Christian he sees his work take on a new richness of meaning. This is illustrated in a powerful paper entitled '*A Physicist in the Presence of the Cross and the Resurrection*' by Professor G. Ludwig, of the Department of Physics at the University of Marburg-Lahn in Germany. He wrote:

> 'God himself as son of the father became as a man like us, in order to humiliate himself on the cross even unto death. Every sign of arrogance on our part about our so-called achievements ought to collapse at that point and we should concede that even the findings of physics are not our own achievements, but a gift, and our contribution in work and effort is but trivial in comparison.'[60]

The Christian in science, therefore, needs a mind immersed in the Bible and a mind 'renewed by Christ'. Gone are the old ambitions, fears and failures. He seeks to think God's thoughts and to see things from God's perspective. The old ego is gone and new life in Christ has come. He is no longer driven by the transient priorities of the world, but by a desire to fulfil the eternal purposes of God.

The life of Christ is central to Christian ethics because his teaching guides us into the will of God and because his life gives us the grace to submit to it. The Christian life is a life of complete harmony with God. David Cook wrote:

> 'It is a life of loving God, our neighbours as ourselves, and one another as Christ himself loved. The Kingdom life is not a do-it-yourself affair, for it is to share in the benefits of Jesus' life and work. By his salvation, healing and restoration, he enables men and women to be transformed and to live the life of God.'[61]

In touch with the world

There is an important role for Christians to play in questioning what is happening in society. As I write, Dr John Habgood, the outgoing Archbishop of York, features in all of the national newspapers for his condemnation of the Internet! He writes:

> 'My nightmare society is a lot of self-centred individuals concerned only with their own fulfilment, sitting all day in front of their computer or television screens, and soaking their minds in increasingly violent and obscene entertainment.'

The response of *The Times* Editorial fascinated me.

> 'Religious leaders have every right to question the impact of science upon culture and morality. In many instances, the effect is positive. The debate on genetic engineering would have been poorer without the interventions of the Church. The laws of war would not have been developed as they have without the reflections of religious thinkers upon new

military technology. Yet Dr. Habgood's apocalyptic tone is misplaced. Any new medium can be used to propagate violent or obscene material.'[62]

Whether or not Habgood was right to condemn the Internet is not really the point. What impressed me is that his comments have instigated an important debate about the use of the Superhighway. It's a good example of Christianity exploring the ethics of technology.

The Christian who is immersed in the Bible, who knows the teaching of Christ, and who lives in a personal experience of Jesus must also be in touch with the real world. Christians must try to differentiate between right and wrong in scientific practice.

The Christian is driven by higher principles than the 'profit motive'. The Christian perspective of the world reaches beyond the insatiable quest for new markets to a more philanthropic view of life. The *People's Creed* written by the African church and political leader Canaan Banana neatly sums it up.

'I believe in the Spirit of Reconciliation;
The united body of the dispossessed;
The communion of the suffering masses;
The power that overcomes the dehumanising forces of men;
The resurrection of personhood, justice and equality;
And in the final triumph of Brotherhood.'

To whom are we responsible?

Behind the ethical dilemmas which scientists face today there lies the question, 'Who owns the planet?' If man is but a steward of the world – to whom are we ultimately responsible? The Bible teaches that all living things as well as human beings are part of God's creation, and are the object of God's redemptive purposes.

As we saw in the previous chapter, human beings are seen

as trustees of nature, charged with the role of protecting and developing the natural world in accordance with God's purposes. Ultimately, anyone working through the implication of Christianity in the field of science-ethics must have this sense of God's ownership of the cosmos, and an understanding of the responsibility which rests on us all in our stewardship of it.

Christian ethics are integral to the work of Christians involved in scientific research. This is not a kind of ethics confined to proof-texts and simple dogmatic formulae for ethical questions. Christian ethics is about wrestling with the mysteries of our world, struggling with questions which bring different answers when cast in different ways, and agonising to know the mind of God when the pressure is on to deliver results. Christians should use their understanding to push forward the boundaries of knowledge for the good of humankind and for the benefit of society. A Christian cannot compartmentalise his ethical standards and his scientific activity.

The Quakers make an interesting case-study of this kind of activity. For centuries, there has been a strong connection between the 'Quakers' and the world of science. The movement was founded by George Fox (1624–91), and some of the main characteristics of the church were its independent view of things, devotion to the Bible, and strong social conscience. It produced many famous scientists and entrepreneurs who made important links between science, technology and business.

The Quaker, John Dalton (1766–1844) was the founder of the chemical atomic theory. Thomas Tompion, the Bedfordshire Quaker clock-maker, played an important role in equipping the Royal Observatory (1676). Abraham Darby discovered in about 1707 that charcoals could be replaced by coke in the smelting of iron.

It is interesting to note that the Quakers' acute business sense led to the harnessing of science and technology in such businesses as chocolate (Rowntree, Fry, Cadbury), biscuits

(Huntley & Palmer), pharmacy (Allen & Hanbury), soap-making (Crosfield), tanning (Richardson), and mining (Pattinson).

Some historians would argue that the 'non-conformist' Christian culture of the Quakers led them to view the world differently. They questioned the 'status quo' and introduced revolutionary ideas into their research, technology and industry.

The Quaker scientists and business community are an interesting example of the link which Christians can make between good science and good ethics. High standards of business practice, care for workers and sensitivity to ethical matters have been hallmarks of the Quaker movement. Their Christian faith impressed upon them a need to transform the world and to make it a better place.

The scientist as priest?

The integration of Christianity and social ethics should be important to all Christians involved in science. If our scientific work is not compatible with the teaching of Jesus, its practice should be seriously questioned.

Some see the work of scientists as having a priestly quality. They deal with matter, and Christianity teaches that God created matter and that he became incarnate within it. When scientists deal with matter they are dealing with the holy.

John Habgood, the outgoing Archbishop of York quoted earlier, was previously a pharmacologist at Cambridge. In a detailed theological reflection entitled *The Scientist as Priest* he argued that scientists have a sacramental role in caring for the world. He concluded:

'. . . some, I hope, will see with new eyes how this messy recalcitrant reality with which we spend our lives wrestling, can be invested with new meaning and dignity and depth as we say over it the words "this is my body".'[63]

Our experience of Christ's love enables us to view the world differently, and to work alongside him for its transformation. John E. Haught observed what happens when Christians come to terms with the picture of a loving, suffering Saviour.

'At a time when our primordial trust has been weakened due to our experience of suffering, mortality, guilt and the threat of meaninglessness, an encounter with this picture is capable of allowing us to trust once again that we are cared for and that reality is not indifferent to our deepest longings.'[64]

Some scientists have taken this understanding of God's love so seriously that they have given their lives in trying to interpret it in practical and sacrificial ways. Blaise Pascal, for example, was a brilliant theoretical physicist and experimenter, but he was also a mystic who worked for the poor in Paris right up to his dying day. In more modern times Simone Weil (1909–43) was an outstanding French scientist who undertook a sacrificial ministry among the poor in France. While we may not all be called to adopt such an alternative lifestyle, those who have done so provide a dramatic illustration of what can happen!

Every Christian engaged in scientific research deserves our love and prayers. He needs the support of a church which will act as a sounding board without being condemnatory or judgmental. The research scientist needs to know that we will not fling proof-texts her way, but engage with her in the struggle. We are willing to share the anguish, to face up to the sometimes seemingly irreconcilable problems of conscience and to seek the mind of God together.

The Christian engaged in research needs to develop a Christian mind; a mind which engages with the four great chapters of the Bible's story; a mind renewed and in touch with the living Christ; and a mind in tune with the many grey areas of science ethics, a mind in touch with the world.

Perhaps scientists are the priests of the new age. Perhaps they need to be reminded that what they touch is sacred, and that, one day they will have to defend their activity before the author and finisher, the alpha and the omega!

A new millennium: The future role of science

The age when scientific discovery heralded a new utopia for the world seems to be over, and many observers suggest that society is less and less confident that science will solve its problems. J.C. Sawhill, writing in *Science* concluded that there is 'public disillusionment' and 'today's more jaundiced view' of science has meant that 'faith in the beneficence of scientific endeavour and the promise of technology has been steadily eroding.'[65]

Reviewing the decline of budgets in the United States for scientific research (with the exception of cancer-related projects, energy creation and other immediate 'quality of life' applications) Dr. Roger Sperry observed:

> 'It becomes increasingly evident that the prime, urgent need of our times is not for more science and improved technology, medical, agricultural or otherwise, but for some new ethical policies and moral guidelines to live and govern by that will work against overpopulation, pollution, depletion of resources, and so on.'[66].

Visions of the future in art, literature and cinema have often depicted a world of approaching apocalyptic chaos. Such visions have a place in reminding us that the way we live today determines the world that exists tomorrow.

Ridley Scott's spectacular movie *Blade Runner* starring Harrison Ford does seem to depict the apocalyptic nightmare! It is a haunting vision of the city of Los Angeles in the year 2019. The nightmare has become reality. The city is a misty rain-drenched ruin, where technology has run amok. Ford plays an embittered bounty hunter rounding up 'replicants', products of genetic engineering, humans without souls, which are seeking to overthrow their masters in the cosmic colonies.

What I found most disturbing was the way in which the director projected forward current trends, exposing us to the nightmare scenario of urban decay, violent behaviour, desperate isolation and loneliness, and the breakdown of normal patterns of family life and human relationship. It is clear from the drab, dirty city that technology has failed to bring the new utopian dream. Much of the chaos has itself resulted from a technology running out of control.

If we are doing no more than stripping the world of its resources and putting off the evil day when overpopulation finally catches up with us, we are not being stewards under God. How can we avoid the apocalyptic nightmare? What is the role of the scientist in the development of the future age? Technology for technology's sake is no longer a viable reason for scientific advance. John Haught argues that scientists should be at the forefront of evolving a more human and dignified planet.

> 'Christians hold that faith in God is inseparable from the building of true human communities bound together by a love that respects the dignity and worth of each individual.'[67]

To act and pray for the future

The 'green' movement has done a great deal to make us understand that what we sow, we will surely reap. A simple examination of what we're doing to the very air we breathe drives the point home. Motor vehicles, industrial plants and waste disposal systems pump all kinds of pollution into the air.

Sulphur dioxide contributes to acid rain, nitrogen oxide causes smog, carbon monoxide reduces the amount of oxygen that can be carried by the blood, volatile organic compounds are released as gases when benzene escapes from exhaust pipes, and hydrocarbons are released when fuel isn't completely burned. As a result ozone is created when sunlight plays on smog, and millions find it difficult to breathe.

Little wonder, then, that the number of children admitted to hospital for asthma in the UK has more than doubled since 1980. One in seven children now suffers from asthma, and in some inner city areas one child in three suffers from this awful affliction. Nearly a third of the UK population lives in areas where European health standards for air quality are breached.

As the world turns through another millennium the need for action on the environment grows ever more urgent. When God commanded Adam and Eve to 'fill the earth and conquer it' the Hebrew word 'Radah' used implies that they were to fulfil the role of a 'viceroy'.

We are called to be trusted servants, representing the King, and responsible to him for all that we do. We are expected to be completely just, and not to exploit the earth. We are stewards who are working in harmony with nature, and we are ultimately responsible to God for our management of human affairs and of creation.

One of the most haunting experiences I have ever had happened when I was in Manila, in the Philippines. I was seated in a fast-food burger bar munching my 'Big Mac' when a child appeared at the window in front of me. He pressed his face hard against the glass, and gazed at me with big dark eyes. This child had an emaciated body. His cheeks were drawn, his belly swollen, his eyes huge. He was, quite literally, starving. I put down my burger. I couldn't eat. Here was I, enjoying fast-food in air-conditioned luxury, to the beat of well-known western music, whilst a child was starving on the other side of the glass. I had fast food, and he had no food at all.

Later the same night a local church leader walked me past the lines of neon-lit strip joints, clubs and brothels, to a tiny coffee shop sandwiched between two nightclubs. He pushed the door ajar, and I counted twenty-seven children asleep on the table, under it, and in every inch of the darkened room. 'Child prostitutes,' he whispered, 'they come to the church refuge when there's no other place to go.'

In this apocalyptic nightmare of a world filled with fast-food bars and nightclubs, a world of hi-tech entertainment and international travel, yet a world which allows children to starve on the city street, or be used as prostitutes for the gratification of evil men, one has to ask where the technology's utopian dream brought us. Perhaps *Blade Runner* isn't about tomorrow, but today.

Christians have a major role to play in tackling the enormous problems facing civilisation in the next millennium. Trusteeship of the planet is at the heart of our faith, and we must learn how to communicate responsibility towards the planet and its dwindling resources. Sir John Houghton, recently awarded the Gold Medal of the Royal Astronomical Society, and a leading environmental scientist wrote:

> 'Science and technology have a large role to play in the solution of the enormous problems we face. But on their own they are inadequate; they can even be harmful. Value judgements are also required . . . a religious person would want to be more specific and say that we are acting on behalf of God – we have a God-given responsibility to look after the Earth. Further, in facing the problems involved we are not meant to act independently of God but rather in partnership with him, as indeed the word "stewardship" implies.'[68]

The pursuit of Christian ethics in science is a key area for Christian action in the new millennium. In every field, from transportation to genetic control, Christians must work for a greater sense of stewardship of the created and of responsibility to the Creator. We must persuade the scientific community to ask more important questions than 'will it work?' or 'will it make money?' There are more pressing needs than satisfying man's never ending quest for knowledge.

We must pray that researchers will recognise that they must work with the Creator rather than against him. The biologist Arthur Peacocke noted that it is when scientists engage in the work of 'co-creating' and work 'with the grain' of the Universe that they truly discover the will of God.

> 'The enterprise of co-creating with God as creatures, could also provide the basis for a new mode of interaction of science and Christian theology. . . . This, it seems to me, is the

direction in which we should be looking for a sound basis for that "creation centred" spirituality and a theo-centric ecological ethic which many in our contemporary society are now seeking.'[69]

A major consultation of the National Council of Churches in Washington DC in 1980 unanimously agreed that what the world needs is a new approach to theology, one that can promote the values of conservation, renewable energy, and the like. It would seem that a union of science, ethics and religion is what is required to help solve the problems of the new millennium.

New technology can lead us to decide for a happiness based upon higher productivity, a better standard of living, a host of labour saving-devices, or hi-tech electronic forms of entertainment. What good are these in a world which can no longer support us, in a society starved of human relationship, in a community which abuses its children, or in an environment spoiled forever. What good is technology when the milk of human kindness has run dry?

What the world needs now is love, a love with flows from discovery of the love of God. How we can stop the wastage of natural resources? When will we recognise the basic human need of personal spirituality? Christopher Kaiser, who is qualified in both natural science and theology wrote:

'The time may even come when an operational faith, supported by a religious community and its creeds, will provide insight and inspiration for the pioneers of new scientific developments as it did in Western Europe from the Middle Ages to the nineteenth century.'[70]

I do not believe that Christianity is a form of escapism from the awesome problems that confront the human race. It's not a distraction from a world that's spiralling out of control. Christianity is the driving force for the new world. Christians in science should be working for wholeness not materialism, for a world of better qualities of human life and not greed.

The challenge for Christians is to move into the grey areas of confusion and to shine on them the light of God's love and righteousness. Christians in science have an exciting but challenging role for the new millennium. They hold the key to the future, and the key is the will of God!

5

Does Science Do Away with God the Creator?

(David Wilkinson)

What place for God as science gives us more and more information about the origin of the Universe? This is a question which is often heard and has been brought to popular attention through the work of Stephen Hawking in recent years. In this chapter we will examine the Christian doctrine of creation and the centrality in it of Jesus Christ. We will then suggest ways in which this can be reconciled and indeed interact with modern science.

While sitting on a railway platform I overheard the conversation of a couple sitting next to me. They were doing a crossword, most of which was far above me. However, one of the clues intrigued me. It was, 'Where the Universe came from'. The woman paused, and said 'Two words, the first has three letters, the second has four and both words end with the same letter'. Two possible answers came to my mind. One was 'Big Bang', the other was 'God said'. Both I will argue are valid answers to the question, but which one was appropriate to the crossword puzzle depended on the surrounding context.

Where do I come from?

'Let's start at the very beginning, a very good place to start'. Julie Andrews may not have been seeing further than 'doh, ray, me', but she was summing up a fascination with origins!

A few years ago, the director James Toback, interviewed a large number of people on the topic of origins. These interviews were cut together into the movie, *The Big Bang*.[71] At the beginning of the movie a scientist talking about the Big Bang is interspersed with people being questioned on how the Universe came into being. Some their answers were fascinating:

'You're asking me? I have no idea. You better ask my brother the priest!'

'The cosmos? I know exactly when it started, February 18th 1934, coincidental with my birthday.'

'There must have been something, some, you know ... cosmic soup or whatever they describe it, some little speck happened to ignite and made some other stuff, but I could easily be persuaded that that is more irrational than thinking something happened out of nothing ... because I cannot imagine nothing.'

'The beginnings in my own life were always beginnings of love and I hope that this is somehow what happened when the cosmos came into being.'

'If there's an isness, it always was is, and it always will be is, and it ain't going to be less than or more than.'

'I don't really wonder an awful lot about that ... I think more than likely, it probably didn't have a beginning, or maybe ... I don't know.'

'I believe that everything that is written in the Bible is true.'

There is obviously a wide range of opinion! It is interesting that the only person who says she does not think a lot about it, turns out to be a philosopher! It is a clever opening to the movie. Side by side you have the competing claims of science and religion, certainty and uncertainty, the personal and the cosmic.

People are obsessed with origins. One of the first questions in the meeting of new people is, 'Where do you come from?' Such a question of course can be asked on a more fundamental basis. We are asking such questions to locate ourselves in relation to others. To ask where did the Universe come from gives ourselves understanding a reference point from which to work.

It is within such a context that both science and Christianity attempt to speak. Scientists aim to provide an accurate understanding and description of the Universe, in terms of its origin, its structure and its evolution. This is called cosmology. Christianity speaks of the Universe as the creation of a personal God. The popular myth is that the two are in competition and only one can win. But is this true?

In order to answer this we need to look behind the popular myth and see what cosmology and the Christian doctrine of creation really say.

What does the Bible say about the origin of the Universe?

I suppose that when talking about the origin of the Universe, the obvious place for many people to go to find out about what the Bible says is the opening chapter of the book of Genesis. Of course much has been written on Genesis 1 and its relation to modern science.[72] However, such an approach can ignore the many other places where the Bible talks about creation. In particular, passages in the New Testament while reflecting the truths of Genesis 1, also build upon it. One such passage is contained in Paul's letter to the Colossian Christians. Here he writes of Christ:

> 'He is the image of the invisible God, the first born over all creation. For by him all things were created; things in heaven and on earth, visible and invisible, whether thrones or powers or rulers or authorities; all things were created by him and for him. He is before all things, and in him all things hold together. And he is the head of the church; he is the first born from among the dead, so that in everything he might have the supremacy. For God was pleased to have all his fullness dwell in him and through him to reconcile to himself all things, whether things on earth or things in heaven, by making peace through his blood shed on the cross.' (Col 1:15–20).

What then is Paul's understanding of creation? We need to notice a number of things:

1   The Bible is rarely interested in cosmology for its own sake

This is a great drawback for people trying to write a book on the relationship of science and religion! Galileo said of the purpose of the scriptures, 'The intention of the Holy Ghost is to teach us how one goes to heaven, not how heaven goes.' The biblical teaching about creation is located in passages which are concerned with other issues as well.

Such a passage is the one quoted above. It is part of a particular letter to a particular congregation at one point in its early history. Many PhD theses have been written on why the letter was sent, and scholars still disagree. It is clear however that false teachers were affecting the church, putting Christ down and encouraging the young Christians to follow them to get knowledge and take part in certain religious practices. What is unclear is just who these teachers were – a pagan cult, a sect of Judaism, an early form of what later became known as Gnosticism or those who were seeking to win over Christians to the observance of the Jewish law?

In response to this false teaching Paul reminds the church of who Jesus is and what it means to follow him. Thus this passage is 'Christological', that is it speaks about the person and nature of Jesus. Paul rubs this in with the repeated phrase 'He is.' His argument is very simple. Aiming for Christian maturity, he says, if you understand who Christ is, you do not need secret knowledge or particular practices for he is supreme in all things. Part of that supremacy is in creation.

This is an important reminder. Even the Genesis 1 text is not solely concerned about how the Universe came into being. Many scholars have pointed out that it is more like a hymn of worship, wanting to encourage the reader to respond to the God of creation. When we also recognise that the Bible's teaching is contained in a particular cultural setting, and uses different literary styles we should pay careful attention to what the Bible is actually saying rather than what we would like it to say.

2 The creator God is revealed in Jesus

There is a story about a little girl who was painting a picture. Her mother came to her and said, 'What are you painting?'

'A picture of God', the little girl replied very seriously.

'But', said her mother, 'no one knows what God looks like.'

'Well' said the little girl, 'they will when I've finished my picture!'

The little girl, of course, was answering one of the most fundamental philosophical questions of all time. If God exists, what is he like? And how do we know?

One starting point is to say that if God is the creator of the Universe, then the Universe itself might be able to tell us something of what the creator is like. Now we know that the Universe is pretty big. Our Sun is one star in a collection of 100 thousand million stars which make up the Milky Way galaxy, but this galaxy is only one of 100 thousand million galaxies in the Universe. If the Universe is created, then this leads us to the obvious conclusion that God is very big, most probably infinite! But, by seeing that God is so great, you introduce a great problem. How can our small, finite minds ever come near to understanding what an infinite God is like?

Or you might say that God is a God of order. One of the most amazing things about the Universe is that underneath its massive complexity, science has discovered many simple and elegant laws. The Universe has an order to it, which we call the laws of physics. Is this a picture of what God is like? Some like Professor Stephen Hawking believe that to discover this order is to know the mind of God. But does that mean that God is simply a great computer or even a mathematical equation?

Of course, there are other things about the world. Events such as the bombing in Oklahoma City are a graphic reminder of the freedom that humans possess to abuse others. This leads to the question of did God mean it to be that way, or is he prepared to do something about it?

In the light of these type of questions, Paul makes the most startling claim. It is that at the heart of the Universe there is not just a mathematical theory, but a divine personality. The order of the Universe does not have its origin in the laws which describe it, but in the creating and upholding work of a personal God. Furthermore that very same divine personality is focused supremely in the man Jesus of Nazareth. For how can the great God be known by human beings? Only if God reveals himself to the human mind, in a way that the human mind can understand.

That is what Jesus Christ is all about. He is the 'image of the invisible God', (Col 1:15), the projection of the nature of God into our world. One of the wonders of modern science is the overhead projector! I can write on an acetate with reasonably normal writing. In front of a lecture hall, the audience will not be able to see the writing, particularly if the acetate is placed horizontally on the projector. But once the power is switched on, through an ingenious arrangement of lenses and mirrors, an exact representation or image is projected onto a screen in the vertical plane from which the audience can read the writing. In a similar way, Jesus is the projection of the Creator God into our space time dimensions in a way that makes sense.[73]

In answer to the question, what is this Creator God like, Christians reply he is like Jesus. That is in the life, death and resurrection of Jesus, God has spoken about himself. When Philip asked Jesus the fundamental question, 'Lord show us the father and that will be enough for us,' Jesus' simple reply was, 'Don't you know me, Philip, even after I have been among you such a long time? Anyone who has seen me has seen the Father' (Jn 14:8–9).

Such staggering claims were often difficult to understand for the early church. How can Jesus be both man and God? Some said he was just a good man whom God used. But Paul will not allow that. He sees Christ as the one in whom all the fullness of God was pleased to dwell (Col 1:19) and that the death of Jesus was the achievement of God himself (Col 1:20).

By fullness Paul means that there was nothing whatever of the Godhead that was not in Jesus. He was not less than God.

Others then suggested that Jesus was just God but not really human. Someone who walked three feet above the reality of human existence. Paul will not allow that either. In verse 22 of the same chapter he talks of Christ's 'physical body', as a reminder that this Jesus was fully human. Paul will not allow anything less than that the fullness of God was in the man Christ Jesus.

How can the infinite God be known? Paul is saying that only in Christ can the creator be fully known. Now that is not to say that we know everything about God. If we did, then we would be gods ourselves. Nor is it saying that God does not reveal himself in other ways. It is simply saying that this creator does not hide as a mystery, but appears within our very humanity.

3 At the heart of creation is Jesus Christ

Deep within the wisdom literature of the Old Testament, God's creative activity is described in terms of the figure of 'wisdom' (Prov 8:22). This was a way of expressing, in a figure of speech, certain aspects of God's creative character. In 1925 the scholar, C F Burney, pointed out that Paul in Colossians applies to Jesus everything that could be said of this figure. Paul is saying that at the heart of creation is not a divine attribute but a divine personality.

Christ does not displace the God of the Old Testament, he makes him known. Those things said about Israel's God, Yahweh, are now said about Jesus. He is 'the first born over all creation' (Col 1:15). This could mean the first thing in the Universe created in time, as Jehovah's Witnesses would have us believe. But in its context, and with everything else that Paul writes about Jesus, he is not the first created being but the phrase signifies the supreme rank or that he is prior in importance.

Christ is not simply a part of the created order 'for by him all things were created' (Col 1:16). A better translation would actually be 'in him'. Creation is the activity of God the Father in the Son. Jesus is not solely responsible for creation but the Father and Son are together in creation just as the eyes and hands of a workman are together in making an object.

However, not only do all things have their origin in Christ, 'in him all things hold together' (Col 1:17). The verb is in the perfect tense indicating that 'everything' has held together in him and continues to do so, that through him the world is sustained and prevented from falling into chaos. What is the source of the unity, the order and consistency of the Universe? Paul is suggesting that it is to be found in the continuing work of God in Christ.

The main thrust of these verses is that the whole of the created order in space and time owes its origin and continued existence to Christ. What does this all mean?

What is the purpose of creation? The philosopher Wittgenstein towards the end of his monumental *Tractatus* wrote, 'The solution of the riddle of life in space and time lies outside space and time'. Science can never answer such a question. After 173 pages of Stephen Hawking's A *Brief History of Time,* in which he gives his scientific understanding of the origin of the Universe he is still left on the last page with the question 'Why?' Paul is saying that Christ is the clue to this purpose.

Is science a Christian thing to do? This understanding of who Jesus is, means that to explore the order of the Universe in research science, or to exploit that order in technology is a 'Christ'-ian thing to do. So often the Christian church in recent years has alienated scientists or been suspicious of scientists. But to do science is to explore the work of Christ.

The church often talks about 'full time' Christian ministry and really means clergy, pastors and evangelists. But scientists and engineers are also in 'full time' Christian work! Does the church support and value them as such?

What should the world be like? In Christ we see the principles of how the Universe is meant to be. It is almost that Christ is the 'template' of creation, that is, the values which Jesus demonstrated of self giving love, faithfulness, generosity and the importance of relationships are the way the Universe is made and meant to be. A medical scientist once wrote:

> 'Jesus is Lord. It is he by whom all things exist, it is he who spiralled the DNA helix, who choreographed the genetic quadrille in cell division, who scored the hormonal symphony and who heals the wounds we bind up. And by looking to this Lord, the doctor of Galilee and sustainer of every galaxy, we can day by day calibrate our behaviour.'[74]

Is your God too small? This passage is a reminder that our picture of God can often be too small. Paul was saying to these young Christians that they did not believe in some small god of a cult but the one through whom all the Universe is made. One of the great understatements of the Bible occurs in Gen 1:16 when the writer says, 'He also made the stars.' It is a kind of 'by the way', he also made the stars! The billions of stars in billions of galaxies, all were made through him. Christ is not only the one who comes to us with open arms of welcome, he is also the God of all creation.

One of my favourite Christian songs is an old East African marching song which has the lyrics:

> What a mighty God we serve!
> What a mighty God we serve!
> What a mighty God we serve!
> What a mighty God we serve!

Now there is not a lot of imagination to those lyrics, but Paul would agree!

4 God has no competitors in creation

Paul makes a point of listing in verse 16 all the power structures of the Universe. Commentators disagree on whether he is referring to supernatural powers such as demons or angels, or to earthly powers such as governments. What is clear is that he is saying that all these things owe their existence to Christ. He is not a rival to pagan gods but is supreme in all things.

Christians have traditionally believed in the doctrine of 'creation out of nothing'. That is, God did not use stuff that was already around, like lighting the blue touch paper of a 'blob' of matter that was already there to make a Universe. If something already existed out of which he made the Universe, then God would not be absolute. The doctrine itself emerged as late as the end of the second century in the thinking of Theophilus of Antioch and Irenaeus. However, here in this passage Paul is reflecting such a doctrine. Christ does not use things already there or have to overcome rival forces, he brings into being all things.

This seems to be the assumption behind Genesis 1:1 in terms of 'In the beginning, God created the heavens and the earth.' This clear understanding of creation coming from nothing rather than a pre-existent matter underlies other biblical passages such as Proverbs 8:22–26 and John 1:1–3.

That means that creation itself is distinct from God. He is related to it as he sustains it but he is different to it. As we have become more aware of problems with the environment, some have talked of respect for nature, and some have even gone as far as speaking of nature as divine. The Bible itself is quite clear that nature is not divine. However, it is to be valued as the creation of God.

5 The God of creation is also the God of new creation

Have you ever watched a television programme with great interest but missed the end because of an interruption or a videotape coming to an end at the wrong time? To fully understand a story, you need both the beginning and the end. The same is true with the Christian understanding of creation. God's work does not stop at the end of the first chapter of Genesis!

Paul in fact gives a parallel between creation and new creation. Both are accomplished by the same agent. The one who is creator is also redeemer. Of course this is based in the Old Testament view that Israel's God, the one who delivered them from Egypt, is also the creator of the whole Universe (Isaiah 40:12–31).

The parallel here is expressed in the phrase 'firstborn'. It is used as 'over all creation' (Col 1:15) and then 'from among the dead' (Col 1:18). Jesus is not only the beginning of the creation, he is also the beginning of the new creation. This is demonstrated by his resurrection. His resurrection is the beginning not only of the new age, but will be followed by the resurrection of believers.

One of the key aspects of this new creation is reconciliation. Although the Bible acknowledges this creation to be good, it also acknowledges that something has gone wrong. This is due to men's and women's separation from God, wanting to be god for themselves. That sin is overcome by Jesus' death on the cross which achieves reconciliation. Paul's use of 'blood' (Col 1:20) gives a model for this reconciliation in the idea of sacrifice.

However, his canvas is large. Another parallel between the One who creates all things and reconciles all things emphasises the universal scope of God's action. No one is outside God's reach. It also has the sense of bringing the entire Universe into a new order and harmony. Indeed within other passages of the New Testament, God's purposes are seen to go beyond this Universe into a 'new heaven and new earth' (Rev 21).

It is somewhat unclear quite what the physical relationship of the old creation and new creation will be. However, the key to it is the resurrection. The resurrection of Jesus is seen as the 'first fruits' of God's purposes for all creation (1 Cor 15:20–28). It is a model of what the new creation is to be like. Therefore, it is significant that the evidence within the New Testament suggests that the resurrection body of Jesus had both *continuity* and *discontinuity* with his life before the cross. The continuity is reflected by:

- the risen Jesus is recognised by the disciples (Jn 20:19–20)
- he eats fish (Lk 24:42–43)
- he shows them his hands and side (Jn 20:24–31)

However, although they know that this is the same Jesus he seems to have different physical characteristics:

- on the road to Emmaus two disciples walk miles with Jesus without seeming to recognise him (Lk 24:13–35). There have been many suggestions why, including the sun was in their eyes, their eyes were filled with tears or that they were too frightened to look around! Surely what Luke is telling us is that Jesus was somehow different
- he did not seem to be confined to space and time, such as appearing in rooms with locked doors (Jn 20:19–20)

Jesus in some way has transcended the constraints of his earthly life. He is the Jesus that the disciples knew but he is different. We might expect this same mixture of continuity and discontinuity as characteristic of the new heaven and earth.

The Christian understanding of creation therefore is not just about what happened at the beginning. Just as you cannot fully understand a film by seeing only the opening credits, Paul is keeping together the beginning, the decisive moment of the cross and pointing forward to the future fulfilment.

It is this total centrality of Christ which is the thrust of Paul's counter attack against the false teaching affecting the Colossians. In our own day it can also undergird the Christian's view of science. As long ago as 1898 Bishop Handley Moule wrote of this passage,

'It connects the remotest aeon of the past with him. It connects the remotest star detected by the photographic plate with him. It bids us, when we feel as if lost in the enormity of space and time, fall back upon the Centre of both – for that centre is our Lord Jesus Christ, who died for us. In him they hold together. . . With that same dear name, the explorer of physical secrets can consecrate his laboratory, remembering that Christ is the ultimate Law of compound and cohesion, while he is the Saviour of the soul.'[75]

Well, you might say, that all sounds very good, but where's the evidence? Why take this view seriously at all? Paul does give an answer to that important question. Submerged beneath the breathtaking cosmic view of Christ is a simple but mindblowing phrase. It is this, 'Christ is the first born from among the dead, so that in everything he might have the supremacy'. Paul is saying that there is an event so radical, so inexplicable in terms of science, so unexpected and yet an event recorded by the evidence of history. It is the resurrection. It is the confirmation of the picture.

I could describe my wife as 'kind, generous, considerate, beautiful, witty', and many more things. That would give you a picture of what she is like. But to confirm that picture you would have to meet her, to enter into some kind of relationship with her. In the same way the confirmation of this picture of God is not just the historical evidence for Jesus, but the invitation to a relationship with this risen Jesus.

How does science describe the beginning?

If this is what the Christian faith says about origins, what does science say? The progress in cosmology over the centuries has been due to a number of important elements. The belief in order in the Universe as described by mathematics began in the Greek culture, was strengthened by the Christian world view and led to laws such as Einstein's theories of relativity. These laws enabled scientists to probe back in time in both the physical and biological spheres. In all of this, observation took a leading role in determining how good the suggested models were.

So what would be a typical picture of origins as given by science today? Roger Forster, leader of the Ichthus

Fellowship and Paul Marston who lectures in the history and philosophy of science, set out a typical picture of origins as it would be generally accepted in any science faculty[76]:

- between 8–18 billion years ago our Universe (including its time and space) began with a 'Big Bang' – giving rise to a Universe which has been expanding ever since
- the matter arising from the Big Bang began a complex system in which stars and galaxies form and develop in predictable ways
- our solar system formed some 4–5 billion years ago (the earth about 4.6 billion) by mechanisms still under dispute
- life began with tiny micro-organisms 3.5–4 billion years ago. Multicellular animals began around 700 million years ago. Land colonisation began some 425 million years ago
- varieties of living creatures evolved. Mutations in genetic codes (DNA) were occasionally beneficial and enabled the animals bearing those mutated genes better to survive and pass the genes on. This process of natural selection led to accumulated changes and a divergence of life forms increasingly specialised to fit particular niches in a natural environment itself subject to change. This process is broadly reflected in the sequence of fossils in the geological strata
- mankind evolved, probably through a fairly narrow 'bottleneck' in geologically recent time, with modern man appearing sometime in the last 100,000 years

Forster and Marston acknowledge that this is our best picture at the moment, if it may not be in the future. Furthermore, it does not answer all of the questions, there still are problems with each of the elements in the above account, and there continue to be disagreements between workers in the field. Finally, some Christians dismiss it all, arguing that the Bible gives a literal historical account of the creation of the world some thousands of years ago in a period of six days.

These are important issues. What we need to do is to be

clear about the evidence on which these statements are based. It would need a book considerably longer than this one to cover all of the above statements, so in the following we will focus on one area and look at some of the questions in detail. This may give us an insight into the scientific method, some of the questions that still remain and how one can view it as a Christian. The area we will choose will be the Big Bang.

What's the evidence for the Big Bang?

Sherlock Holmes was a great scientist! Not in the sense of discovering any new physical law but in his method. By combining his powers of reason with his skill for observation (and granted one or two disguises down the way!) he would solve the puzzle and catch the criminal. In many ways a good detective is similar to those who study the origin of the Universe.

Today scientists believe that they can give a good description of the Universe from the present day to an age when it was only a fraction of a second old. At that stage the Universe was an incredibly dense mass, so small that it could pass through the eye of a needle. From that point it expanded very rapidly in what is commonly called the Big Bang. American poet Robert Jeffers writes,

> 'There is no way to express that explosion – all that exists roars into flame, the tortured fragments rush away from each other into the sky, new Universes jewel the black breast of night and far off the outer nebulae like charging spearmen again invade emptiness.'[77]

Within the first 1000 seconds of the expansion, hydrogen and helium atoms are formed. Over the next billions of years, clouds of hydrogen gas collapse under gravity to form galaxies of 100 billion stars. Stars continue the process of creation as they progress from their birth to their death. The energy they produce is due to burning of hydrogen into helium and other elements such as carbon, oxygen and nitrogen. When stars exhaust their fuel, they shed these elements into space to be used for the next generation of stars. Thus, on this picture, the carbon that forms human beings is literally the 'ashes of dead stars.'

However, someone may ask how do you know this is true? No human being actually saw the Big Bang! Of course scientists only appeared on the scene fifteen billion years after the Big Bang, never mind the first few seconds. Furthermore, some of these things are so beyond our everyday experience, how do we know that they actually happened?

Now we are helped a degree by the fact that we can look back in time. This is because light travels at a finite speed of 300,000km per second. Therefore, when we look at the most distant galaxies, we see them as they were ten billion years ago, as it has taken that length of time for their light to travel to us. This is useful as we can check our models of what we think the Universe was like ten billion years ago against our observations of what it was really like. However, for various technical reasons we can never get right back to the start.

Cosmology is a little different to the rest of physics in that it deals with a unique event which happened in the past. You cannot get a Universe into your laboratory and set off a Big Bang to study it! Due to these problems, this is where Sherlock Holmes comes in.

When Holmes reaches the scene of a crime he has not seen the crime happen, but he tries to reconstruct what actually happened from the evidence he finds. Indeed, the conclusion he is forced to might often stretch Dr Watson's imagination, but if that is what the evidence requires, so be it. Cosmologists in a similar way observe various pieces of evidence and then try to give the best reconstruction or 'model' of what happened billions of years ago.

Three pieces of evidence are particularly important:

An expanding Universe Early in this century the astronomer V M Slipher observed that the light from other galaxies displayed a phenomenon called redshift. This occurs when light is emitted by an object which is moving away from us. Edwin

Hubble then measured the distances to these galaxies and found that the further away they were, the faster they were moving away from us. This was the first piece of evidence that the Universe was not static, but expanding. And if it is expanding, it must have expanded from somewhere.

Today, the redshift of galaxies is taken as evidence of the Big Bang. However, Sherlock Holmes would never build a case on only one piece of evidence and so cosmologists looked for other clues!

The background radiation In the 1940s the physicist George Gamov and his colleagues had predicted that if the Universe started off with a Big Bang then a certain kind of radiation should fill the whole of space. This was not found until 1965, and indeed was found rather by accident. Arno Penzias and Robert Wilson were attempting another experiment altogether when they detected this microwave background radiation or 'echo' of the Big Bang.

For most cosmologists, it was this piece of evidence which provided the main support for the Big Bang model.

The amount of helium in the Universe Most of us do not know a lot about helium, apart from that it is the gas which fills balloons and if you breathe a little of it then your voice becomes rather entertaining to others! However, it is a very abundant element in the Universe. In fact about a quarter of the gas in the Universe is helium. This figure which we have been able to measure quite accurately in the last twenty years is the amount we would expect if the Universe began in a Big Bang.

The Big Bang under attack!

Of course these three pieces of evidence cannot prove the Big Bang, but in a sense nothing can. Detectives can only give the best reconstruction of the crime; they may sometimes get it wrong. In reality, there is never a Dr Watson going 'Gosh Holmes, that's quite brilliant,' but other detectives questioning whether the interpretation of the evidence is the best. The questions they raise may because of new evidence, or a piece of the jigsaw that they feel fits in another way, or it may even be because of prejudice or the attempt to get on with their career.

So it is with the Big Bang. New clues are always coming to light, and other questions remain which do not quite fit into the jigsaw. Scientists are also real people. Some have prejudices about what they would like to be right, others will occasionally publish articles to be controversial and to get their name heard.

Over the last thirty years where Big Bang has occupied centre stage, it has been attacked on many fronts. It is a testimony to its endurance, that although somewhat modified it still stands strong.

Problems with philosophy

In the 1960s Fred Hoyle, Herman Bondi and Tom Gold argued against the Big Bang for reasons that had perhaps more to do with philosophy than with the evidence. They believed that the Universe should be the same at all times. Of course they meant its main features, such as the number of galaxies in a particular part of space. This should be the same whenever in the Universe's history that you measured it.

Now if the Universe had a beginning and was expanding from a point this would not be true. Their solution was to replace the Big Bang, with a Universe of no beginning where matter was continuously being created throughout space. This would force the galaxies apart in order to explain the redshift. As the theory developed Hoyle proposed mechanisms to explain the microwave background and helium abundance apart from the Big Bang.

What was the motivation for such a view? They were trying to avoid ours being a 'special time'. They wanted it to be a time like any other in the Universe. In addition, Hoyle disliked the Big Bang for its inelegance, and one cannot escape that this steady state theory was preferred by atheists such as Bondi on the grounds that he thought the Big Bang supported theism.

Does all of this show, as some argue, that science is controlled by philosophical assumptions and prejudice? If Hoyle can explain the evidence as well as the Big Bang model, how do we know which one is right? This does remind us that evidence can be used for two different conclusions. But it is fair to say that the vast majority of the scientific community reject the Hoyle model because it does not fit the evidence so well and because some of the explanations (such as for the microwave background) are rather contrived. Judgements are made in accordance with the criteria we outlined in Chapter Three. In the end philosophical prejudices still have to be controlled by observations and the criteria of what is a good theory.

Problems with new observations

The Big Bang model has both been supported and questioned on the basis of new observations. In 1994 two pieces of work hit the headlines in claiming that the Universe was only half the age that we previously thought. By measuring distances to galaxies in a large cluster called Virgo it was possible to give an estimate of the age of the Universe. The answer that was obtained was 7–8 billion years compared to the fifteen billion years that had been thought previously. Although one may reply what is a few billion years between friends (!), the difficulty of this result is that it is generally accepted that the age of certain stars is much longer than 7–8 billion years. So how can the stars in the Universe be older than the Universe itself?

Does this mean that Big Bang falls in ruin? Not quite, as science is a little more complex than that. Many things could have produced this somewhat odd result. There are many technical reasons why these studies may have underestimated the age. Alternatively, the standard model of the Big Bang may not be the best, or we could have got the ages of the stars wrong. Furthermore, how do we balance the evidence that we already have for the longer age of the Universe against these new observations?

What happens in practice is that the scientific community goes back and checks the results, looks to see how the theories can be modified and weighs the evidence on which model is best. This indeed may mean that the model is thrown out and a new one brought in, but one needs patience rather than jumping to conclusions.

This is very important to remember, particularly for those who attack scientific models like the Big Bang. After outlining the evidence for the Big Bang at a public meeting, I was sent some articles by a concerned fellow Christian who was arguing against the Big Bang. They were popular science articles highlighting what was thought to be a major problem with Big Bang. At that time, the Cosmic Background Explorer satellite (COBE) had shown results that meant that there was no evidence early in the Universe that galaxies were able to form. The articles had been sent to make the point that this disproved the Big Bang. I replied that this was a problem, but that we needed to be careful about absence of evidence and there was still a lot of evidence for Big Bang. The reply to that was not complimentary!

What I did not realise was that two days later on the morning of 24th April 1992, the morning newspapers were dominated by headlines referring to COBE's discovery of ripples, or the seeds in the early Universe out of which galaxies eventually would form. COBE had taken more data and just as we notice more details the more we look at something, so the ripples had appeared. This supported the Big Bang model.

The following week I received some more papers, this time quoting an eminent astronomer's reaction to the COBE discovery. It was from an interview that he had given on the day that the news broke. He had wisely cautioned that there may be other interpretations of the observations, but this had been seized upon in the article which was headlined 'Professor X doubts Big Bang'. I knew Professor X personally and I knew he did not question Big Bang at all! All he was doing was showing scientific reserve in the face of recent observations.

We need to be careful about manipulating recent observations or popular news stories to support our theological convictions. C H Spurgeon in a famous remark when asked to defend the Bible replied, 'I would rather defend a lion.' If Christianity is true, then the truth does not need to be bolstered by half-truths.

We need to be clear that there are a number of scientific problems remaining with the Big Bang. What is the nature of much of the mass of the Universe which we know is there, by its gravitational effects, but at the moment we cannot see? Is the Universe 'too lumpy' for our current theories of how galaxies form? What is the age of the Universe? Science takes time to answer these and other questions.

Still today, articles and newspapers will appear with headlines questioning the Big Bang. But it needs to be said that the model of the Big Bang is the best model we have at present of how the Universe began. It may have to change in some minor respects, but most cosmologists believe that the evidence we see confirms it as a very good picture of what actually happened.

Does the Big Bang contradict the Bible?

However, in acknowledging the Big Bang model to be reasonable, this highlights the question of does it contradict the Bible? Now in Paul's letter to the Colossians there is no difficulty. The Big Bang could be the mechanism through which Christ brought the whole Universe into being.

However, although all Christians agree that God is the source and sustainer of the whole Universe, there is disagreement on how he does it. The disagreement has often become polarised over how to interpret the first chapter of the book of Genesis. Some argue that it is literal scientific history and therefore in stark contrast to the Big Bang. They say that the Bible speaks of a creation some thousands of years ago. This time scale is calculated from tracing back the family trees to Adam through the rest of the book of Genesis. Others equally convinced about the authority of the Bible, see the first chapter not as scientific history at all, but as expressing the truth of God's creation without regard to time-scale or process.

In the often heated debate, those who hold to a literal understanding of Genesis are portrayed as dogmatic obscurantists, while those who do not are accused of rejecting the Bible and even blasphemy. In the light of such debate, the arguments tend to revolve around details rather than seeing clearly the key issues.

I remember going for the first time to a great Cathedral. I was fascinated by the decorations and memorial stones on the walls and floor. I would have spent all my time looking at such details, if my teacher had not said, 'David, look up!' There above me was the most magnificent roof.

We can at times get so wrapped up in the debate that we do not think clearly and therefore miss important issues. Let me suggest that we need to be clear on the following:

Be clear that this is not a question about the authority of the Bible

The way that you view Genesis 1 in relation to the Big Bang (or any other model of creation) is a question about how you interpret this particular part of the Bible. A man once went up to an academic who had just given a talk on the Bible and said, 'Of course, Professor, you interpret the Bible, I just obey it!'. But as James Packer, one of the world's leading evangelical thinkers has often emphasised, the Bible is only authoritative when interpreted correctly.

Over its whole history the Christian church has held a number of interpretations. Long before modern science and the Big Bang, Augustine understood the 'days' of Genesis not to be taken literally. Some have argued that the days represent 'ages', while others have held that the writer of Genesis 1 just was not interested in science or time scale at all. Remembering all of this should be a caution to humility. We can hold to the infallibility of the Bible while acknowledging that our interpretation of it is fallible!

It also helps us stay clear of the argument which goes 'if you don't believe Genesis 1 you cannot believe the rest of the Bible.' But this 'slippery slope' argument only works if all the literature in the Bible is of the same type. We know that some is history, some is parable, some is poetry, some is theology, some is worship. What we need to do is interpret each passage on its own merits.

Be clear about what the passage actually says

We need to ask the question, 'What kind of literature is this?' In other parts of the Bible we do this quite naturally. For example, when the lover says of his beloved that 'Your nose is like the tower of Lebanon' (Song of Songs 7:4), we do not assume that the lover is pointing out that the nose is like granite and over forty feet long! We understand that it is a picture to describe how beautiful the nose is!

However, when we come to Genesis 1 it is not so easy. The biologist and Anglican priest Professor Douglas Spanner wrote, 'The tendency to assume that the Genesis account is so simple and artless that anyone can comprehend it at first glance appears to be very widespread.'[78] Many people just use a simple reading of the text. Some will say it is just science. Others will say it is just story without any history. The trouble is that the Bible sometimes does not give up all of its secrets to those who simply want to use it for their own ends. The text itself of Genesis 1 probably is a complex woven fabric of history, poetry, attacks on other beliefs, a song of worship and theology. We must take care not to unravel it and take what we fancy from it. The challenge to Christians who want to be true to the Bible is to work at being true to the text itself.

Be clear that those on opposite sides of the argument hold their positions with integrity

Some scientists hold to a creationist position. They do not do so by closing their minds and having 'faith'. They argue against the Big Bang on the basis of scientific reasons. Or they hold to a position which says that the findings of modern science are accurate but only tell us about appearances. This is the position that says that God made the Universe thousands of years ago, looking as if it is billions of years old. On the other side it must be said that the majority of scientists who are Christians are not convinced by these arguments. Many hold to the Big Bang being the best model we have at the present, and hold this as a picture of how God created. They do not do this by throwing away the Bible. They simply understand Genesis 1 not as a scientific piece of literature but nevertheless true in telling us that behind the creative process is God.

Be clear that one can hold to creation without holding to the seven day 'creationist' position

Many make the mistake of confusing the two. If the Big Bang is the mechanism, then this does not mean that God did not create the Universe. It would be like saying that because we understand how the television works, no one invented it! As we shall see when we look at miracles in the next chapter, just because we can understand how something happens does not mean that God is not acting in that situation.

Be clear that the God who creates in seven days is neither superior or inferior to a God who creates over a time scale of fifteen billion years

Some argue that if you do not believe in a seven day creation you do not believe that God has the power to do it. This is misleading. Arguments could be employed to the contrary in terms of God's glory being shown even more in the intricate and patient care he takes in a fifteen billion year creation. After all, on my birthday my wife usually spends hours baking and decorating a cake. On her birthday I go to the supermarket and buy a cake already made! It is perhaps the one that takes the most time which has more value!

In the light of the above issues, Christians come to different conclusions. We need to be real about this and respect each other. Some argue that the Bible rules out the Big Bang picture altogether. Some while rejecting biological evolution are happy to accept Big Bang. Others are happy to accept both biological evolution and the Big Bang as the mechanisms of how God creates.

Ernest Lucas who holds PhDs in both chemistry and the Old Testament concludes his book *Genesis Today*[79] with the words:

> 'We would expect the Bible , the sourcebook of Christian teaching, to be primarily concerned with questions of meaning rather than mechanism. This turns out to be the case for Genesis 1–11.'

My own position which I have detailed elsewhere,[80] for what it is worth, follows this understanding. Over many years of struggle and delight with the first chapter of Genesis, the text itself forces me to recognise that it is not a science text-book but something more profound. The indications in the way it is written suggest that it is a hymn of creation as part of worship to the Creator. It uses poetry, its main assertions are theological and its purpose is to encourage the reader to worship this great Creator God. This is not to say of course that there is no history within it. It is just to say that we cannot simply 'lift' history from it.

Therefore for me, the Big Bang is currently the best model we have which describes how God did it. Genesis 1 comple-ments that description with the fundamental truth that the purpose, the source of order and faithfulness of the Universe can only be found in this Creator God.

Does Stephen Hawking do away with God?

In recent years, a new aspect of the creation debate has devel-oped following the popularity of Professor Stephen Hawking's *A Brief History of Time*. It has become the coffee table book possessed by many but read by few. Hawking himself has achieved international fame from BT adverts to appearing on *Star Trek*! This is due in large part to his remark-able personal story. Diagnosed with a rare form of motor neurone disease while a young man he now communicates via a voice synthesiser where each word has to be laboriously entered. Yet his mind has probed the very depths of the Universe making him one of the outstanding scientists of our generation, if not of all time.

His name is heard at academic conferences, in church sermons and in meaningful ways in sixth form common rooms. Some use him in attacking God, others use him to support their belief in God. But what does he actually say and what does it mean for Christian faith?

A barrier to the beginning?

Among his many achievements, Hawking has suggested a possible solution to a fundamental problem with the Big Bang. It is, 'What happened at the first moment?' This is a great frustration for scientists. As we described earlier, modern science uses its knowledge of the physical laws to reconstruct a model of what happened in the past. Using this method, science has been extremely successful. It can describe what the Universe was like billions of years ago. In fact it can describe what the Universe was like when it was only one second old! If that is not mind blowing enough, our present models of physics can take us back to an age when the Universe was:

$$\frac{1}{100,000,000,000,000,000,000,000,000,000,000,000,000,000,000} \text{second}$$

We write this as 10^{-43} second to stop us having to write out all of the zeros. Now that is a very small fraction of a second, but it is not zero! You would have thought that scientists would be happy with such an achievement, but no way. It is like the video switching off after watching a thriller for six weeks a second before the killer is revealed. Scientists want to know what it was like at the very beginning.

Why do our current theories break down? This is a complicated story. The first is a limitation to Einstein's theory of General Relativity. Earlier this century Einstein gave a brilliant description of gravity. He suggested that we imagine the space and time of the Universe to be rather like a stretchy fabric.

To illustrate this, get a couple of friends to hold the ends of an elastic bandage keeping it taut between them. The surface of the bandage will be horizontal. If you now place a heavy object somewhere on the bandage it will be no longer flat. The object will have altered the shape of the surface of the bandage. If you now take a smaller object like a golf ball and place it near to the heavy object, it will run down the slope into the heavier object. In a very simple way, this is what Einstein was saying about gravity. The presence of objects distorts the space-time of the Universe and smaller objects are attracted by larger objects. It is a brilliant description of gravity and works everywhere in the Universe, apart from at one time. At 10^{-43} second it breaks down. This is because at this point, the whole of the Universe is very small.

In the simple demonstration, it would be equivalent to me jumping on the bandage. I am a very massive object in a reasonably small space. The effect would be catastrophic! We would all end up on the floor and the demonstration would break down. In a similar way the theory of General Relativity is unable to cope with the situation and the model breaks down unable to give us any meaningful description.

The second reason why our science breaks down is that at this point the Universe is so small that it should not only be described by relativity, it should also be described by quantum theory. But the two theories at the moment are incompatible. Rather like, the leader of the Scouts and the secretary of the women's group who meet once a year at the village fete. For the rest of the year it does not matter that they don't get on, for they each have their respective areas of influence, but when they both want the table at the door then there is trouble! General Relativity describes the Universe on the large scale of planets and stars, while quantum theory describes the small scale of atoms. The only place they meet is when the whole Universe is at the atomic scale.

All this means that current scientific theory is unable to give a description of the initial conditions of the expansion of the Universe.

A beginning or not a beginning . . . that is the question?

Do we need God to 'fix' the initial conditions of the Universe? If science is unable to describe the initial moments is this where God comes in to set the Universe off?

What Hawking does is to suggest a possible way of uniting quantum theory and gravity to describe the beginning of the Universe. One of the results of this is, to put it bluntly, that he describes how the blue touch paper of the Big Bang lights itself. The core of Hawking's theory, in John Barrow's phrase, is that, 'Once upon a time there was no time.'[81] Hawking is saying that the Universe does have a beginning but it does not need a cause for in the theory the notion of time melts away. This is very difficult to understand or illustrate.

When we talk about beginnings we often have in our minds the image of causes. The beginning of the 100 metres is the moment the starter's gun causes the athletes to run out of their blocks. There is a moment in time when we can say the race started, and we know what caused it. We often think of the Big Bang in such a way. At a particular point God reached out his hand and lit the blue touch paper of the Big Bang.

If Hawking is correct, then his picture of the beginning of the Universe is very different. Imagine taking a sweater with a pattern on it and unravelling the wool so that at the top the pattern remains while at the bottom the wool is in individual strands. Then ask the question where does the pattern begin? Well, it must begin somewhere, for there is a pattern at the top but no pattern at the bottom. But we cannot identify an exact starting point. The pattern emerges out of the strands. Hawking's Universe in a similar way emerges from a fluctuation in a quantum field. No cause as such is necessary.

It must be stressed that there are many scientific difficulties with Hawking's theory:

- there are other proposals on how to deal with the problem of the laws breaking down
- Hawking actually does not have a full theory, he makes his suggestions on the basis of this is what the theory would look like if he had a full theory.
- it is difficult to know whether quantum theory can be applied to the whole Universe

Much more work is needed on these and other problems.

What is there left for God to do?

If Hawking is right, does God become redundant? I remember sitting in a conference when the full implications of Hawking's theory hit for the first time. Up to that point I had argued against many of my atheist friends on the basis that the Big Bang proved God. If they said that the Universe had come from a Big Bang, I would reply with statements like, 'But who set it all off?' Although very simplistic it was often very effective!

Indeed I was echoing an argument that had been used for centuries in the Christian church. The argument goes something like this. Everything around us has a cause which happens before the event. So if I see a cricket ball flying towards me I know it must have been hit or thrown by somebody or something. If we say that our Sun was made by a contracting ball of hydrogen gas, and the hydrogen was made in the first few moments of the Big Bang, then surely something caused the Big Bang. Such an argument is still used today in many Christian books (although it is presented in a little more academic way!).

What Hawking is saying is that such an argument does not work with the beginning of the Universe. Quantum theory deals with events that do not have causes. By applying quantum theory to the Universe this removes the need for a first cause. No one is needed to set it all off.

In fact, if I had remembered my philosophy, Hawking was reinforcing earlier criticisms of the 'first cause' argument.

Augustine had pointed out many years ago that the Universe was created with time not in time. Therefore to ask the question what came *before* the Universe is attempting to use the concept of time before it came into existence! In addition, the first cause argument derives from the question whether the Universe is a thing or event. Now it is easy to say every thing has a cause, but is the Universe a thing or event? Surely it is the totality of all events and things. To argue that everyone has parents does not mean that humankind has a mother!

Seeing my knock-down proof for the existence of God crumbling, I found myself more and more worried that this somehow disproved God. However, a Christian Professor of Physics at the same conference took me aside and pointed out that Hawking was doing away with a 'god', but this was not the Christian God.

My use of the 'who lit the blue touch paper' argument had led to a very different god to the God of Christian belief.

The 'god of the gaps'

There is a tendency if science has a gap in it to insert God as the explanation. In Newton's theory of how gravity described the orbits of the planets, he needed God to occasionally reposition the planets. As understanding of the orbits grew, science filled in this gap, so when Laplace was asked whether he needed God to fill such a role he replied that he had no need of that hypothesis.

As scientists explained more and more about the Universe, so people looked more and more desperately for unexplained gaps in the knowledge of the natural world in order to say, 'Scientists do not understand that – it must be God.' But as the gaps became smaller and smaller so God was pushed out into irrelevancy.

The first moment of the Universe was the last big gap. It was as if 'God' was sheltering in its safety, but then Hawking came along and said out! And why not? The God of the Bible does not shelter in safe gaps.

This 'god of the gaps' happens because of the mistake of

confusing different types of explanation. As we saw in Chapter Three, science and theology can give different but compatible explanations of the same thing. Some atheists such as Richard Dawkins believe that once you have a scientific explanation then that is all you need. Some Christians believe that there are some things in the natural world that science should not explore because they are 'God's work'. Both are wrong.

The Bible understands that the whole Universe is the result of God's working. He is at much at work at the first 10^{-43}second as at any other time. A scientific description of that moment in time does not invalidate it as being the activity of God as any other event.

Charles Coulson, the Oxford scientist, who many years previously had criticised the 'god of the gaps' approach wisely wrote: 'When we come to the scientifically unknown, our correct policy is not to rejoice because we have found God; it is to become better scientists.'[82]

The god of deism

Coupled to this, such an attempt to prove the existence of God often leads to a picture of God closer to deism rather than the Bible. The deists believed in a god who set the Universe off and then went away to have nothing more to do with it. Nothing could be further from the God of the Bible. Creation is not a single initial act, but the bringing into being and moment by moment keeping in being of the whole Universe.

So I suggest that Hawking should be welcomed by Christians. Whether his theory is correct or not we shall have to wait to see, but what he demonstrates is the inadequacy of a deistic god of the gaps. This should drive Christians back to their biblical roots where they will find a very different God!

What does Hawking not explain about the Universe?

In the same breath as Stephen Hawking you will hear the phrase 'a theory of everything'. People often interpret this as

Hawking attempting to get a theory which would explain literally everything in the world. This is not the case. Hawking is attempting to construct a theory which explains how the Universe develops with time and its initial conditions. Such a theory if possible would never be able to explain by itself our weather for example (see the next chapter for a discussion of chaos).

It must always be remembered that apart from the scientific questions it leaves unanswered, it also leaves a number of other important questions about the Universe unanswered. Science is successful because it limits its range of questions. There are many other questions left:

Why the Universe?

Hawking himself states, 'Although science may solve the problem of how the Universe began, it cannot answer the question: why does the Universe bother to exist? I don't know the answer to that.'[83] The philosopher Leibniz had asked many years ago, 'Why is there something rather than nothing?' This is not to resurrect the first cause argument, it is to recognise that the purpose and meaning of the Universe lie beyond science. The Christian will argue they find a natural answer in a personal God.

Where do the scientific laws themselves come from?

If the Universe emerges as a quantum fluctuation, we need to ask where quantum theory itself comes from? Where does the pattern of the world come from and how is it maintained? This is not a 'god of the gaps' argument as science itself assumes these laws in order to work. There is a long tradition stretching back to Newton who saw the laws of the Universe as the work of the divine law giver. Kepler was 'carried away by unutterable rapture' as the correlation between orbital periods and mean diameters, which showed that the planets moved in elliptical orbits, was disclosed. Once again the Christian will argue the Creator God is the natural answer.

Why is the Universe intelligible?

Why can anyone write a chapter like this? You might say it is not done very well and not very intelligible. Nevertheless, the very fact that we have been talking about the Universe so early in its history is a testimony to the extraordinary ability of human minds to explore and understand the Universe at such a fundamental depth. Why can we do this?

Some writers, including John Polkinghorne, suggest that the natural answer is that there exists a Creator God who is the basis of the order in the Universe and the ability of our minds to understand it.

What is our significance in the Universe?

In Chapter Two we saw how the Universe seems to be finely tuned to the existence of life and the way we respond with awe. These insights do not prove God but may point the way towards him. What is our place in the Universe? For some it is a terrifying question. Pascal wrote, 'The eternal silence of those infinite spaces strikes me with terror... When I consider the short extent of my life, swallowed up in the eternity before and after, the small space that I fill or even see, engulfed in the infinite immensity of spaces unknown to me and which know me not, I am terrified and astounded to find myself here and not there.'[84] The Christian can answer with words also written in response to the vastness of the Universe:

> 'When I consider your heavens,
> the work of your fingers,
> the moon and stars which you have set in place,
> what is man that you are mindful of him,
> the son of man that you care for him?
> You made him a little lower than the heavenly beings
> and crowned him with glory and honour.' (Ps 8:3–5)

Is there a way to know the Creator God?

Kepler wrote, ' There is nothing I want to find out and long to know with greater urgency than this. Can I find God, whom I can almost grasp with my own hands, in looking to the Universe, also in myself.'[85]

We began this chapter by suggesting that the answer to all these questions is actually to be found in Jesus Christ. They are questions which are raised by science but are unable to be answered by it. Sir Robert Boyd, Emeritus Professor of Physics, at the University of London, in commenting on whether Hawking's theory would show us the mind of God, wrote, 'The missing data in Hawking's analysis of the "Mind of God" is the mind of One "who made Himself of no reputation", whose love is unconditional and whose "Name is above every name."'[86]

This centrality of Jesus Christ is summed up in Professor Boyd's own poem originally written for Holmbury Parish Magazine at Christmas:

'In the beginning', long before all worlds
Or flaming stars or whirling galaxies,
Before that first 'Big Bang', if such it was,
Or earlier contraction; back and back
Beyond all time or co-related space
And all that this and all that ever was
And all that yet will be; Source of the whole,
'In the beginning was the Word' of God.

The Word of God; Reason, Design and Form,
Intelligence, Whose workshop spans the stars
Expressed within the Cosmos and alike
In what seems chaos; He Who works as much
In randomness as order, Who to make
Man in His image scorns not to create
By patient evolution on a scale
Of craft divine which dwarfs a million years.

Who is this God, that bows Himself to see
The puny wonders of this little speck

Of cosmic dust that we have named our Earth,
The toy volcanoes and the restless sea
That splashes from His bucket like a drop
And still a captive to the circling Moon
Flows and recedes, purging polluted shores
Or sending tidal torrents up the Severn?

Who is this God, that circles either pole
With fluorescent light, an arctic dawn,
Whose rain makes little sparks and tiny cracks
That we call thunder storms, this God Whose plan
So shapes the atoms that they must combine
To give dust life and then to feed that dust
With inorganic substance to create
By DNA a pattern like its own?

Who is this God and can this God be known
Within the confines of a human skull,
A litre and a half of mortal brain
Whose interlinking neurones must depend
On chemistry and physics in the end
For all that Man can know or comprehend?
Can Man know God eternally enthroned
Throughout all space and in the great beyond?

The mystery of being, still unsolved
By all our science and philosophy,
Fills me with breathless wonder, and the God
From Whom it all continually proceeds
Calls forth my worship and shall worship have.
But love in incarnation draws my soul
To humble adoration of a Babe;
'In this was manifest the love of God'.

Still Jesus comes to those who seek for God
And still He answers as He did of old,
'I've been with you so long, how can you say
"I don't know God, oh show me God today?"
When you've met Me you've seen the eternal God
Met Him as Father too, as He Who cares
And loves and longs for men as I myself.
I am the Christmas message. God has come.'

(*Quoted by permission of Professor Boyd*)

6

Can You Believe in Miracles in a Scientific Universe?

(David Wilkinson)

Many people doubt the existence of miracles because science rules them out. In this chapter we first of all take great care in defining miracles according to the Bible, and then see that the scientific objections against miracles are weak. Indeed, a scientist approaching the resurrection would find strong evidence for its truth.

A little boy was asked at his school to write an essay on birth. He went to his mother and asked how he was born, and she replied, 'You came as a gift from God.' He then asked his grandmother how his mother was born. She replied, 'The stork brought her.' He then asked his grandfather how his grandmother was born. He replied, 'She was found under a gooseberry bush.' When he handed in his essay it began with the words, 'In my family, there has not been a natural birth for three generations!'

What is natural? And what is a gift from God? The subject of miracles often divides people between two poles. There are those both inside and outside the church who are sceptical of the existence of miracles while there are others who will genuinely testify that miracles have occurred. It has to be said however that many of the arguments employed on both sides to support their respective cases are somewhat suspect and often are somewhat confused on what miracles actually are.

Yet today there is a resurgence of interest in miracles.

Within the church, the beginning of the Pentecostal movement earlier this century and the charismatic movement of
the last thirty years have raised the profile of the 'supernatural'
in many churches, and particularly raised questions about
healing. John Wimber's 'power evangelism' argued that the
western church had lost spiritual power because of the domi-
nance of a view that 'we live in a Universe which is closed off
from divine intervention, in which truth is arrived at through
empirical means and rational thought.'[87] It is only by being lib-
erated from that world view that signs and wonders can be
brought back into the practice of evangelism. 'Health and
wealth' gospels argued that God does not want his followers
to be poor or ill, and so miracles from Ferraris to immediate
cures for indigestion should be claimed by faith. In the 1990s,
the movement of the Spirit commonly known as the 'Toronto
blessing' has again raised the question of the supernatural in
both the Christian and secular media.

A mystery about miracles

We need to recognise right from the start that there is always
a mystery about miracles. I was once playing golf with a friend
of mine who was a very confident atheist. In the morning
round I had been fortunate enough to get a three at a crucial
hole which swung the match in my favour. In the afternoon we
came to the same hole with the match finely balanced again.
After two shots he found himself on the green while I was still
150 yards short. He turned to me and said, 'If you get a three
here, I'll repent and believe in God!' I somewhat nervously
got out my seven iron and addressed the ball with desperate
prayer! I hit the shot, the ball bounced once on the green and
then went straight into the hole! The trouble is that he didn't
keep his side of the bargain!

Now there are a whole number of questions about this. Was
this shot a miracle? Of course, if you knew just how bad I was
at golf then you would probably say that it was. But no physical law was broken. Was it just a coincidence? But why did it

happen just at that moment rather than any other since! William Temple once said, 'When I pray coincidences happen, when I don't they don't!' Was this an answer to prayer, and if so why was not my friend compelled to believe?

The questions get more serious when I contrast this story in my mind with another. During my first appointment as a minister I went to see a lovely lady who had just been diagnosed with cancer. She was nearing the top of her profession, enjoying an excellent marriage with many years ahead. She was a fine Christian who was active in the church. Over the next few weeks, I and other church leaders prayed for her healing. We prayed in the name of Jesus, we laid hands upon her and anointed her with oil. As the time went on, her faith stayed firm but her body deteriorated until she died.

Many Christians have had such experiences where we have prayed for people who have not been miraculously healed. Inevitably, the question for me was why God had apparently acted on a rather insignificant golf shot, when he had not apparently acted to heal the cancer. Now of course, he had acted, in the sense that as the lady died she had a lovely sense of the peace and presence of God. However, the question still remains.

In many ways one of the major difficulties with miracles is not scientific, although in this book it will be the science which is our primary concern. One major problem is that if God works by miracle why does he not do it more often? Why does he intervene to provide a Christian with a parking place when he does nothing about the Holocaust?

Many philosophers and theologians have attempted to answer such a question. Christians need to acknowledge that there may never be a full answer to this question and therefore there will always be an element of mystery to miracles.

The question however we examine closely in this chapter is the belief that science makes miracles impossible. This is a widespread statement amongst those who both hold a Christian faith and those who argue against it. To examine whether it is true, we first need to be sure what we mean by 'miracle', and then to be sure about the science.

Is the Bible a book of miracles?

It is undeniable that the Bible is a book which unashamedly records events which are by any definition miraculous. Furthermore, the miracles are an intrinsic part of the story. Jesus turns water into wine at a wedding. John as he records this act of Jesus suggests that there is a certain extravagance about it, for it seems Jesus produced between 120 and 180 gallons of wine at a party where most of the guests had already had their fill! (John 2:1f) Elsewhere, Jesus apparently defies gravity and walks on water (Mark 6), feeds 5000 men plus unnumbered women and children on five loaves and two fish (Mark 6:30f) and heals those who are sick (Mark 6:56f). Even these acts seem almost insignificant alongside the virgin birth and the resurrection.

The biblical writers record these stories in a natural and at times almost matter of fact kind of way. It is not enough to immediately dismiss this 'matter of fact' way on the basis that the biblical writers did not know modern scientific laws and therefore saw no problem. It might be the case that Peter had no understanding of Newton's Law of Gravitation or Archimedes' Principle, but as a fisherman on the Sea of Galilee he knew it was unusual for people to go for a stroll on the surface of the water!

It is worth noting at this point that there are within the Bible a wide spectrum of cases which are commonly called miracles. Some are clearly not at odds with our known scientific laws. Finding a coin in the mouth of a fish, is highly improbable in the statistical sense, but does not contravene a known law (Mt 17:27). They could be rare but natural events. However, others such as water into wine, and the resurrection do seem to go against our current understanding of the regularities in the Universe.

The writers show little interest however in how these things happen. One of the few exceptions is the parting of the Red Sea which delivers the people of Israel out of the hands of the Egyptian chariots. This is understood to be due to a strong east wind (Ex 14:21). It reminds us that we must be careful not to draw too big a distinction between what we commonly call the 'miraculous' and other events. What is important is their meaning or significance.

John's Gospel, of all the parts of the Bible, emphasises this aspect. John calls the miracles 'signs' and they are intricately woven into the story and structure of the Gospel. The signs are coupled together often with the great 'I am' statements. Thus, the feeding of the five thousand is the sign of Jesus' statement 'I am the bread of life.' It points towards and embodies Jesus' claim.

What is the purpose of miracles in the New Testament?

Miracles were acknowledged by the early church to be central to the ministry of Jesus. In the first sermon on the day of Pentecost, Peter says,

> 'Men of Israel, hear these words: Jesus of Nazareth was a man attested to you by God with mighty works and wonders and signs which God did through him in your midst as you yourselves know' (Acts 2:22 RSV).

It is clear that they were integral as part of the story, not novelties to show how clever God was. But what role did they play? It is difficult to give a short answer to that question. Various answers are given in the New Testament:

- the raising from the dead of Lazarus was 'for the glory of God' (Jn 11:4)
- it was also a demonstration of the compassion of Jesus (Jn 11:33,35,38)
- in John's Gospel miracles are a demonstration of Jesus as the Son of God (Jn 20:30)
- the healing of the blind man is an acted parable of the way that Jesus will soon open the spiritual eyes of the disciples (Mk 8:22–26, Mk 8:27f)

- other miracles seem to reveal things about Jesus and the Father such as the right to forgive sins (Mk 2:1–12)

The common theme is that these actions are more than just acts of mercy, or pointers to the divine origin of Jesus, or to attract the crowds. They are first and foremost signs and indications of the fact that the messianic age had arrived in Jesus. That is, they are a dramatic demonstration of God's reign, or the arrival and character of the Kingdom of God through Jesus.

Jesus' own understanding at the beginning of his ministry was that his words and deeds would go together. He went to his home synagogue and claimed that the words of Isaiah were now fulfilled (Lk 4:18–19).

'The Spirit of the Lord is on me, because he has anointed me to preach good news to the poor.
   He has sent me to proclaim freedom for the prisoners and recovery of sight to the blind, to release the oppressed, to proclaim the year of the Lord's favour.'

These words set the scene of what is to happen in the rest of Luke's Gospel and indeed in what Luke records of the ministry of the followers of Jesus in Acts. The Kingdom has arrived, characterised both by the preaching of good news to the needy and by the performance of mighty works. At the centre of the arrival of the Kingdom is Jesus himself.

Later in Luke's Gospel this is re-emphasised. In controversy with the Pharisees concerning the source of Jesus' power in casting out demons, Jesus replies that his casting out of demons is a sign of the presence of the Kingdom (Lk 11:20).

Noticing that the miracles are not just an added extra but very much part of the story is very important for our understanding. CS Lewis wrote,

'If you are writing a story, miracles or abnormal events may be bad art, or they may not. If, for example, you are writing an ordinary realistic novel and have got your characters into a hopeless muddle, it would be quite intolerable if you suddenly cut the knot and secured a happy ending by having the hero left a fortune from an unexpected quarter. On the other hand there is nothing against taking as your subject from the outset the adventures of a man who inherits an unexpected fortune . . . Some people probably think of the Resurrection as a desperate last moment expedient to save the Hero from a situation which had got out of the Author's control . . . (but) Death and Resurrection are what the story is about; and had we but eyes to see it, this has been hinted on every page, met us, in some disguise, at every turn, and even been muttered in conversations.'[88]

How does the Bible view the laws of nature?

Basic to the biblical view is that all events are God's events. Creation is not seen as a mechanical model apart from God, which he makes and then waves good-bye. All events owe their existence to him. Therefore, so-called 'natural' events such as the Sun shining (Mt 5:45) are not only because of 'the contraction of a ball of molecular hydrogen under gravity to a point where at the centre the temperature has risen so that nuclear fusion of the hydrogen into helium begins, thus halting the gravitational collapse while emitting photons of electromagnetic radiation which penetrate the atmosphere of the Earth', but because of God's constant activity. Whether it be grass growing (Ps 104:14), rain falling (Mt 5:45), mist rising (Jer 10:12) or the path of the Sun (Ps 19:4–6), all are seen as part of God's sustaining activity.

In this way there is no hard and fast distinction between the 'miraculous' and what we would call natural events. Creation is not like a clock which God winds up and allows to run its course independently, occasionally intervening by poking his fingers into the mechanism.

Science searches for patterns in the world. We call those patterns the laws of nature. They describe to us what normally does happen. Michael Poole helpfully likens scientific laws to a map of how the land lies. As the lie of the land determines the shape of the map, so our observations of the Universe determine the form of the laws. He goes on to contrast this with an architect's plans. These plans are not descriptive but prescriptive in that they show what ought to take place. Many people make the mistake of seeing scientific laws as architect's plans, telling us what should or should not happen. Of course they do have the ability on the basis of what happened before to lead us to expect certain things, but they do not make these things happen. The map has to be changed by what is really there.

The laws of science are a description of God's regular activity in sustaining the Universe. As I sit writing this paragraph on that wondrous thing called a personal computer, the software gives to the screen and to the keys I press some regularity and order. The software enables me to see what I am writing and I know which parts of the screen to click on in order to change the font, the size, the background colour and how to save all that I have been writing. For most of the time that I write, I do not think a lot about the software, but without it I would not be able to use this computer to write. If there was not a constancy to the software, that is, if it was changing all of the time, the task would be impossible. In fact it is only when something unusual happens that I notice the software. If I press a key by accident which does something unusual (like scrapping a whole day's work!), then I recognise the role of the software in maintaining the environment.

God is the one who maintains the consistency of the laws of physics as they are a reflection of his 'upholding all things by his word of power' (Heb 1:3). If God did not have a faithful relationship to the Universe then there would be no patterns, no regularities, no laws of physics. The Universe would be a place of physical anarchy!

What then is a miracle?

It has always been difficult to define miracles. However, on the basis of what we have seen from the Bible, we might broadly say that a miracle is something unusual which catches attention because of its nature or its timing and is intended by God to be a sign of his activity and power.

This is quite a contrast to the popular view, which is that a miracle is something scientifically impossible. In fact, the word miracle is not really a biblical word. The three main words used are 'signs', 'wonders' and 'mighty works'. Noting this, it frees us from seeing miracles as events of supernatural origins which break the scientific laws. The Bible encompasses a wider set of events. The order and vastness of the Universe can be seen as signs of God's work which leads to wonder. The parting of the Red Sea, due to the wind, by the nature of its very special timing is a mighty work which does not go against the laws of nature.

Miracles are those events that are intended by God to be special signs of the fact that he is present in the world and is in control of it. As a scientist in astronomy you are always dependent on others. Many observations are now done by satellites and the observations are 'packaged' by a team of scientists often elsewhere in the world. This means that they send you the observations and the computer software to display the data on your computer screen. Some years ago the data from one particular satellite had a little surprise to it. Occasionally and without warning, when you displayed the satellite's photograph of a particular part of the sky, a small silhouette of the Starship *Enterprise* appeared in the picture! Assuming that this was not real(!), the team who had written the software had included in the program a routine which randomly displayed the *Enterprise*. It certainly reminded you of who wrote the software!

Can a miracle prove God?

There is a strong tradition in the history of the church of appealing to miracles as recorded in the Scriptures as the foundation of religion. For example, Samuel Clarke in his 1705 Boyle Lectures argued that Christianity was proved by signs and miracles. It is the same argument that exists today, in the way that some Christians will say 'come and see people healed at this meeting and this will prove to you the existence of God.'

However, there are difficulties with such a view. The first is to note that it has a tendency to separate miracles from the rest of the message. Some of the early arguments that saw miracles as proof of Christianity saw the Christian message as moral teaching. You would accept the moral teaching on the basis of the miracles. But as we have seen, that is not the message of the Bible. Miracles such as resurrection are not proof of Christianity, they are Christianity. The message and the miracles go together in the ministry of Jesus.

The second difficulty is to notice that in the New Testament itself, miracles do not lead to proof. Mark records an incident when Jesus was with the disciples in a boat (Mk 8:13–21). The disciples are troubled that they have only one loaf of bread. One can almost hear the frustration in Jesus' voice as he asks them how many basketfuls they collected up after feeding 5,000 with five loaves, and how many basketfuls when 4,000 were fed from seven loaves, events which according to Mark had happened previously (Mk 6:30–44, Mk 8:1–13). Jesus is telling them to do the mathematics! Twelve loaves with Jesus feed 9,000, and that figure leaves out the women and children! Now, work how many are in the boat and as long as there are no more than 750 then we'll be all right with one loaf! 'Do you still not understand?' says Jesus! The miracles by themselves were not enough for the disciples.

Miracles were not proof but clear pointers which people could recognise if they were open to Jesus. For example the evidence for the resurrection cannot prove the truth of Christianity. It may be a pointer that there is more to this Universe than meets the eye, that Jesus is really who he said he was, and that death is not the end. Confirmation of the evidence comes with experiencing the risen Jesus personally which involves risk, trust and commitment.

That is why it is quite natural for my friend not to be forced into becoming a Christian just because of an unusual event like a golf shot. What he makes of that sign will depend on his own judgement and how he views the Christian message as a whole.

Miracles under attack!

For many people it is not enough to argue for the existence of miracles simply because the Bible says so. Strong arguments have been employed against miracles, many of which have been around for a long time.

God cannot work miracles in a scientific Universe

This is an old argument based on science, but is still very popular today. The scientific revolution disclosed a Universe which was regular and predictable. Newton's Law of Gravitation coupled with Kepler's elliptical orbits was successful in explaining the movement of the planets around the Sun. Models were made as toys which represented these motions as a clockwork mechanism. In fact with a knowledge of the laws of physics and the present position of things, it was believed you could tell what had gone on in the past and what was to happen in the future. Edmund Halley's prediction of the arrival of the comet which now bears his name was evidence of how powerful this method was.

Although Newton himself did not take this view, seeing the Universe as a predictable clock is often called a Newtonian world view. The beauty, regularity, and simplicity of the scientific laws were seen as reflections of the order and faithfulness of the Creator God. But this in itself led to problems. If everything could be explained by scientific laws, where was there space for God to do miracles? And if everything was so perfect, being created by God, why did God have to 'correct the mechanism' by doing miracles? Thus influential thinkers such as Spinoza and Leibniz saw miracles as ugly cases where God would be acting against his own wisdom and violating the laws of nature.

Leibniz wrote concerning nature, 'I maintain it to be a

watch, that goes without wanting to be mended by him; . . . God has foreseen every thing; he has provided a remedy for every thing beforehand; there is in his works a harmony, a beauty, already preestablished.'[89]

On the basis of this, miracles of healing and miracles to show God's power were unnecessary because everything was provided for in creation – both for healing and for showing the nature of God.

As our understanding of the scientific laws became greater so this problem became worse. Charles Darwin writing in his *Autobiography* said, 'the more we know of the fixed laws of nature the more incredible do miracles become.'

The evidence for miracles is unreliable

One of the main critics of miracles was the Scottish philosopher David Hume (1711–1776). He suggested that miracles were not recorded by 'men of good sense' but by uncivilised people who knew no better and therefore could not be relied upon. In addition, 'a wise man proportions his belief to the evidence.' As a miracle was rare compared to the evidence for the natural laws of science, then the miracle was not to be believed. Hume believed that in our knowledge of the world, our personal direct experience has priority and the testimony of others is only to be accepted if it fits with our experience. Therefore as most of us have not had direct experience of a miracle, we cannot accept the testimony of others.

It is a moral outrage that God only does some miracles and not others

This is the theological question, 'If God does work by miracle, then why does he not do it more often?' Miracles are often claimed which at best seem trivial compared to the horrors of this world. In fact it is this sort of question, the problem of evil, that has meant that a number of theologians have tried to suggest that God does not act at all in the world. The book *God's Action in the World* by Oxford theologian Maurice Wiles, was nicknamed in my student days *God's Inaction in the*

World. By saying that God does no unusual or particular actions in the world, then God 'is let off the hook' of why he did nothing unusual in the particular case of the Holocaust.

The 'de-miraclising' of the New Testament

These three main problems led to a questioning of the biblical stories. For many the role of science was of prime importance. For example Rudolf Bultmann, the influential biblical scholar, who argued that the miracle stories were not historical accounts was in large part motivated by his understanding that science ruled such things out.

If miracles cannot happen, then what is going on in the Bible? Two main answers were given. The rationalists such as Paulus looked for natural explanations of what appeared to be miraculous. So the 5,000 were fed, not by a supernatural production of bread and fish, but by the crowd, motivated by the example of the small boy, getting out the bread and fish they had been saving for themselves. In this way, Jesus the great teacher could be maintained and his 'miracles' were in affecting human beings' thoughts and actions. However, this kind of approach became extreme. Some have suggested that far from Jesus walking on the water he was in fact walking on a sandbank! It even suggests that the resurrection was in fact Jesus, who was not killed on the cross, being revived in the cool of the tomb.

The other reinterpretation of the miracle stories was given by the German theologian David Strauss in the last century and many others who followed him. This was to see the miracle stories as 'myth'. That is, they were stories created from Old Testament patterns to convey a theological point about Jesus. Stories of Jesus doing miracles were created by the early church to express their beliefs about him. Thus the resurrection did not actually happen, it is a story which tells us that what Jesus lived for will continue, a type of 'Jesus' body lies a-mouldering in his grave, but his truth goes marching on'.

Miracles defended!

Many of these sorts of arguments keep marching on today. If you start from a belief that miracles cannot happen then of course you must explain the miracles away. These arguments can be heard from Bishops, to biblical scholars to bar 'know it alls'. The trouble is that particularly with the scientific objection, the argument is outdated. In fact it is at the latest a nineteenth century argument that does not make sense in the twentieth century.

In our assessment of miracles we need to be clear about a number of things.

Be clear about the science

Why do forecasters get the weather wrong? If Newton's view of the world, which is like a clock, is predictable, then surely we should be able to have perfect weather forecasts not just for the week ahead, but for the next century. Holidays could be planned with utmost precision, cricket matches at Manchester could be timetabled into the few days without rain, and the shipping forecast could be bought in a book for the next hundred years ahead rather than using up all that time on radio!

The trouble is that you cannot forecast in that kind of way. Whether it be the great storm which hit England in 1987, or the fact that it rains when the little sun symbols appear on the television weather map, weather forecasting is a difficult business. Of course, sometimes it gets it right! To be honest, forecasting a week or so ahead is pretty good these days. Studies of global warming give us a good idea of how the atmosphere will change in the long term future. But this is still a long way from perfect prediction. Why is that?

1 Do scientists really know everything?

One answer is to say that we don't as yet fully understand the laws governing the atmosphere. The 'laws' used in the calculations in the Meteorological Office's computer are our current best description of what the atmosphere is really like. As we saw in Chapter Three, science does not give a literal description of reality. Scientific laws are very similar to, but not exactly reality, which means that our current scientific picture will improve with time.

This is a reminder of the folly of saying that our scientific understanding rules out miracles. Scientific laws are the regularities that we have discovered about the Universe, all are subject to possible modification as more data becomes available, and if there are exceptions then we look for an explanation in terms of other laws. It may be that some phenomena appear miraculous not because they are breaking scientific laws but simply because they reflect a deeper truer reality that our present understanding does not reach.

2 *It's more uncertain than we think!*

However, our limited knowledge of scientific laws is not the only reason why we get the weather wrong. Although some may still be stuck in it, science has come a long way from a Newtonian world view which sees the Universe as a vast clock. Over the last century two theories of modern physics have transformed our view. There may not be total agreement on what kind of view they lead to, but they do undermine a mechanistic view. Both question our ability to predict the future in a fundamental way.

Quantum theory This was developed in the early part of this century and deals with the world at the level of atoms and the particles such as protons, neutrons and electrons which form them. It is a very successful theory which has led to major advances such as lasers, computers and even perhaps an understanding of the origin of the Universe.

In Newton's laws, which describe well such systems as the orbits of the planets or the trajectory of a golf ball, by knowing the present position of an object and its movement you could predict where it will be in the future. In the quantum world, that is not possible. You can either know the position of an electron or its movement, but you cannot have both. In John Polkinghorne's phrase this means that the quantum world is 'radically random'. He means by that it is unpredictable and unmechanical.

Some have tried to suggest that it is in this uncertainty that God acts in the world. God has the freedom to 'push' an electron here or there and alter the course of events in the world. The trouble with such a simplistic view is that we are still not terribly sure how the quantum world relates to the everyday world. A golf ball is made of atoms, but the laws which determine its flight are not the uncertainty of quantum theory but the certainty of Newton. It does have a very small probability of spontaneously disappearing in mid flight, but that is never observed (contrary to the claims of some golfers who should be looking more intently in the rough!).

Quantum theory does not therefore give us an easy way of fitting miracles in, or explaining why we have such difficulty forecasting the weather. However, it does severely undermine the assumption that the Universe is a closed mechanism. Reality is a little more subtle than that.

Chaos theory Unlike quantum theory, this theory deals not with matter at the atomic level but with things at an everyday level similar to Newton's theories. What it has helped us to see is that Newton's laws themselves are not able to predict the future in the way we thought. The full implications of chaos theory have only been brought out in the last thirty years mainly due to the advent of computers able to do high speed calculations.

When we look at problems to solve we begin with the easy ones and work up towards the difficult ones. When Newton published his monumental work *Principia* in 1686, he applied his new theory of gravitation to a reasonably simple system, that is two bodies such as the Earth's motion around the Sun. It is simple because you can get an exact answer.

Unfortunately most of the rest of the world is not that simple. Most systems in the world are extremely sensitive to the circumstances around them, so much so that the slightest disturbance will make them act in a radically different way. This means that after a short time a system becomes essentially unpredictable.

We can illustrate this by snooker (or by pool). World champion Stephen Hendry wins his matches on the basis of Newton's view of the world. After having hit the cue ball, the balls eventually come to rest because of the friction of the table, the cushions and the balls themselves. But imagine if there was no friction and after Stephen Hendry made his break at the beginning of a frame we simply let the balls continue to collide into each other and the cushions. Our task would be to calculate using the vast computer that we have brought along with us to the snooker hall, where all the balls would be after just one minute. If you know a little bit about mathematics you might think this is fairly easy. The collisions require no more than school maths to work out. Once you knew the force with which Hendry hit the cue ball, in the case of no friction, you would assume it would be an easy task, more suited to your home personal computer.

You would be wrong. This system, that is the balls moving on a table, is a chaotic system. The staggering answer, is that to accurately predict the position of the balls after only one minute, you need to take into account effects as small as the gravitational attraction (the weakest force) of an electron (the smallest particle) on the edge of the Galaxy which is some 1,000,000,000,000,000 kilometres away![90]

This is clearly beyond the ability of any computer! To know where the balls would be for further than one minute into the future would require computers bigger than the Universe itself!

You may be thinking that here is the scientific reason which explains why you can never pot a snooker ball, especially in front of your friends. But Stephen Hendry can. This is because the uncertainties are relatively small at the beginning but build up incredibly with time.

This is the reason why weather forecasts can be relatively

good in the short term, but get much worse the further ahead you want to predict. The atmosphere is partly chaotic. The laws of physics can be known, but this extreme sensitivity to initial conditions means unpredictable results. This has become known as 'the butterfly effect' after the scientist Edward Lorenz who gave a lecture in 1979 entitled, 'Predictability; does the flap of a butterfly's wings in Brazil set off a tornado in Texas?'

Sir John Houghton, former Chief Executive of the Meteorological Office and co-chairman of the scientific group of the Intergovernmental Panel on Climate Change, writes,

> 'Even if we could observe the state of the atmosphere all over the globe much more accurately than present . . . forecasts of detailed weather conditions would be possible at most some two or three weeks into the future. But forecasts of the average weather or climate, at least in some parts of the world, may be possible much further ahead. And despite the frightening complexity of the whole system, we also have good reason to expect that useful predictions can be made of the likely climatic change due to human activities.'[91]

These words are important to bear in mind. While acknowledging that detailed predictions are out, Houghton is saying that does not mean you can say nothing about the future. Some recent philosophers and theologians have made the mistake of saying that chaos means the future is fully 'open', that is we can know nothing about it. That is not correct. We can predict certain things about the future whether it be chaotic systems or simple systems, but chaos reminds us of the severe limitations of those predictions.

Now what does this mean for miracles? Does chaos give God room for manoeuvre? You see in this way, God does not have problems with 'breaking his own laws'. Because these systems are unpredictable God could work, it is argued, while being undetectable. He could provide an unexpected lighting flash on York Minster while not compromising the physics of weather forecaster.

This may seem attractive in some ways for the defence of miracles. However, if we go down this road, are we saying that God can work only in chaotic systems and not in other ways? Furthermore, we saw earlier that the Bible viewed miracles as signs of God's activity. If God's work is 'concealed' in chaotic systems, is this really a sign?

Such a view still has the danger of falling into the trap of seeing scientific law as prescriptive rather than descriptive. It is saying that in chaos the laws are less prescriptive. As with quantum theory, chaos does not at the moment give us an easy way to understand miracles. But in a similar way, it clearly reminds us that the problem of God violating the Newtonian world view is not such a severe problem as it was the nineteenth century.

These developments have undermined one of the strongest arguments against miracles. If the final picture of the relationship of God to particular actions in the physical world is still somewhat unclear, at least these actions are not ruled out by a now outdated world view which has more to do with philosophy than science.

In the biblical sense, in miracles God is not overriding the order in the world. The scientific laws are regularities of the way God sustains the Universe. The unusual phenomena which amaze us may be part of a deeper unity, rather like the Starship *Enterprise* in the satellite data program. Or they may be, from the human standpoint, deviations from what is regular, while for God they are changes to the regular ordering of natural events.

Be clear about the evidence

Two years ago I was sitting in a seminar group at an international conference listening to talks on different models of the church. Then a Christian minister from Zambia started to talk about the importance of miracles. As an illustration, he told of an incident when he was asked to go by his church to a certain jungle tribe who had killed a previous missionary.

The minister went and attempted to preach the good news to the tribe. However, after a few days the tribe felt that he was offending their nature gods and while he slept some of the villagers crept into his hut, stole his bible and hymn book and threw them into the nearby river. When he woke he was summoned to the chief who told him that he should go away from the village. The minister replied that his books had gone missing and he would not leave until he found them.

As he prayed in his hut he felt God was telling him to go to the river. This he did, followed by some interested villagers. As he again prayed, the Bible rose by itself out of the river and flew at the villagers. They ran screaming back to the village and told the chief what had happened. The chief was so impressed by this that he invited the minister to stay longer and share with them more about this powerful God.

Now I guess you are thinking right at this moment what we were thinking in that seminar group! The minister saw our faces and said, 'I know what you're thinking, but I was there and I can tell you it happened!'

What we were thinking was, did this really happen and on what evidence do we make the judgement? If David Hume was part of the seminar group he perhaps would have made the following criticisms:

1 The reliability of witnesses?

A miracle story from a jungle tribe would fit with Hume's claim of miracles being recorded by uneducated people. Quite how he would have put it to the minister (who happened to have a Cambridge PhD) I would have liked to have seen!

Miracles have been recorded by educated and uneducated people, those who already have religious commitments and those who do not. To write off all witnesses of miracles as uncivilised people is imperialistic intellectual snobbery. To do so in a Court of Law, would be to a produce a court room where instead of promising to tell the whole truth, witnesses would have to first recite Blackstone's Commentary on English law in full to show that they were worthy! Of course the testimony of a witness is given weight according to a number of other factors, but that does not mean writing their testimony off.

2 The difficulty of rare events?

Moving quickly on, Hume would then have remarked that we usually see Bibles fall into rivers, not the other way around. This is certainly true, the Bible is likened to the sword of the Spirit, not a jet bomber!

However, that argument is not convincing. To say that we only believe things that have happened a large number of times, although on the surface this seems to be a scientific statement, in fact would invalidate a lot of science. Of course science looks for regular patterns in the world, and so repeatability of an experiment is important. If one worker claims a particular result then others will try the same method to confirm the result.

However, it is not always that simple. Some scientific events are unrepeatable, for example the origin of the Universe in the Big Bang. This is a one off event and the way of studying it is more akin to history. Evidence is sought which then enables you to construct your best model of what actually happened. Now I know that this analogy with the unusual event of a flying Bible does not quite work, as one may argue that the science that produced the Big Bang is the same as the science we observe today. Nevertheless, one does not dismiss events simply because they are unusual or indeed unique. Whatever the event may be, the scientist will test the evidence and investigate further.

3 I need to see it myself!

Finally Hume would say that as he had never seen such an occurrence himself, this outweighs the testimony of others. But to say that we only accept things we experience ourselves is just obviously untrue. How much do we actually experience ourselves? We are always accepting the testimony of others. Few of us bother to work through the formal proofs of mathematics, but we accept the arithmetic of our bank statements. We use what is generally accepted.

Of course we weigh the testimony of others to an extent by our own experience and the evidence they provide, but there are some events which we never can experience for ourselves. I do not have to spend the millions of pounds necessary to build a particle collider for myself before I accept the testimony of others that an experiment was carried out which demonstrates the existence of particles called quarks within protons and neutrons. Nor do I need to test myself a jet engine before I step inside an aeroplane for the first time.

4 Assessing the evidence

Hume is just too idealistic and pessimistic in how we actually assess evidence. He tends to talk in generalities rather than considering specific events. For many events there is going to be evidence for a particular interpretation and evidence against. What we do is to weigh up the evidence and take a decision. We never get proof, but so what? That is not the way the world is.

Many people today rule out the possibility of miracles because of too simplistic a view of science or evidence. A better 'scientific' approach would be to weigh seriously the evidence for or against particular miracles. This involves looking at different explanations of the same event and seeing which is more likely. For example, can we really agree with the rationalists that Jesus was walking on a sandbank and the disciples thought he was walking on water. It may sound plausible, but think it through. The disciples were fishermen who knew the Sea of Galilee very well. Would they really not know that there was a sandbank there, or even worse let the story of their mistake circulate around their friends and colleagues!

Perhaps the crunch comes on the resurrection. We agree that our normal experience is that dead people do not rise to a state where they will never die again. Do we dismiss this miracle on this basis or are we willing to change our view of the world on the basis of evidence? Other books have gone into such evidence in a great deal of detail. It is enough here simply to note the kind of questions that one would need to examine:

What is the historical basis and reliability of the New Testament which records the events of the death and resurrection of Jesus? Many people have dismissed the accounts as unreliable propaganda written many years after the event. Now of course, the gospels were written for a purpose, and that purpose was not just to record historical fact but to present the good news of Jesus.

However if we discounted all ancient documents on this basis then there would not be much history left! It does not have to be an 'either or' question. The gospels have now withstood years of study and criticism and still their historical reliability can be vigorously defended. There are differences between the gospel accounts concerning details of the resurrection, but far from questioning their reliability, the fact that they are different confirms it. If they were all exactly the same, I guess we would be worried.

Finally as historical documents go of that period, the New Testament books were written down very early. Paul's first letter to the Corinthians was probably written no later than thirty years after the crucifixion. Thus Paul in writing about the resurrection is able to say to his readers that many to whom Jesus appeared are still alive (1 Cor 15).

What is the best explanation of the empty tomb? Christians in Jerusalem who were preaching the resurrection would have been quickly silenced if the tomb was not empty! A curious fact was that there was never in Christian traditions any record of tomb veneration. Now these things seem to indicate an empty tomb but the real question is, why was it empty?

There have been many alternative hypotheses. Some have suggested that in fact on the morning of the resurrection the women went to the wrong tomb! Others suggest that the Romans or Jews stole the body. But all of these explanations fall on the consideration that the easiest way to stop early Christianity (which both the Romans and Jews wanted to do) was actually to produce the body. Others have suggested that the disciples stole the body, but this surely cannot be right for many of them died for their belief that Christ was risen.

Finally, there have been many who have suggested that Jesus did not die on the cross but only passed out. In the cool of the tomb he revived and convinced his disciples he had risen. Well, one could believe that, if you were prepared to accept that a man cruelly beaten, exhausted, crucified, and checked by Roman soldiers who were 'experts' on death, could by himself struggle out under a weight of spices and bandages, roll a heavy stone away, overpower the tomb guards and then convince the disciples that not only was he alive but he was the undisputed conqueror of death! It seems somewhat unlikely to say the least!

What is the best explanation for the claimed appearances of the risen Jesus? The New Testament claims that the risen Jesus was seen over a period of six weeks, on at least eleven different occasions by at least 550 people, many of whom were still alive when Paul wrote to the Corinthians.

Is their evidence to be discounted as simply hallucinations, or did they really meet with Jesus?

What is the best explanation for the church's growth? All the evidence of the gospels is that the disciples were frightened and confused after the death of Jesus. They did not expect the resurrection and even doubted the first reports of the empty tomb. What transformed them into the roaring lions who preached and died for the risen Jesus? And what about the testimony of millions of Christians over 2000 years who in their own experience have encountered the reality and life of Jesus?

Now none of these things prove the resurrection. But taken together they give at the very least strong evidence for the Christian claim that Jesus was raised on the third day. That conclusion cannot be forced. I guess one could always maintain another explanation for all of the evidence. But is it as strong or as comprehensive in the face of the evidence?

On the basis of this evidence, the most reasonable conclusion is, in the words of the theologian Pannenberg, that the resurrection bursts our view of the world. Our view is often that death is the end and that there is no victory for self-giving love. The resurrection points to a deeper reality. It becomes the model, 'the first fruits', of our own resurrection. There is a sense also in the New Testament that the resurrection is an outcome of a spiritual 'law', that self-giving love cannot be held by death, 'But God raised him from the dead ... because it was impossible for death to keep its hold on him' (Acts 2:24).

I was once at a lecture given by a Buddhist monk. At the end of the talk, a young woman said, 'Thank you for the talk, but I have one question. What happens when you die?' The monk scratched his head and replied, 'I don't know, I've never died.' The audience laughed at the clever answer but the young woman would not give up and asked the question again. This time he replied, 'I don't think we can ever know. The only way to know is if someone died, came back to life and told us.' I wish I had stood up at that point and said, 'But Christians know someone who did!'

The evidence is there for each person to make their judgement. There are alternative explanations but one has to weigh the evidence of this unique event. It is to a large extent based on the testimony of others, but it also has an invitation to meet this risen Jesus personally.

Be clear about God's relationship with the world

Sometimes it seems that philosophers make it too easy. In trying to systematise knowledge about the world, their models are just too simple. This is often the case in talking about God. J B Phillips many years ago warned 'Your God is too small.' Of course it is right to think about these things, and it is right to attempt to understand in a logical way how God relates to the Universe. But it should not surprise us if certain things remain unresolved or a mystery to us.

It would remove many problems if God did not do any miracles at all. If God just made the world and then sat back letting it evolve, we would not be faced with such a serious problem of evil. In addition there would not be the need to try and explain how God can alter the manner of his upholding in small ways that may produce miracles and answers to prayer without affecting the overall regularity of the world.

However, the evidence of the New Testament and in particular the resurrection does not leave us with such an easy solution. There is no such solution. Christians are left with an element of mystery which goes beyond our ability to explain. Nevertheless there are a number of important issues that we need to be clear about concerning God's relationship with the Universe.

First, the God of the Bible is both personal creator and redeemer. We noticed this earlier in Paul's letter to the Colossians (Chapter 5). Traditions within the Christian church have often separated the two. Some have stressed God's particular and unusual acts in history to the exclusion of his role in sustaining the whole creation. This has led to a definition of miracles as exclusively something over against the scientific laws.

A man approached me recently asking for prayer for healing. This I agreed to, but also asked him whether or not he had seen his doctor. He gave me a look which communicated that he was worried about my faith and said, 'That's not very spiritual!' But to go to see a doctor is very spiritual! It is utilising the wisdom that is built into the regularities of nature by the Creator God. The skill of the doctor is made possible by being made in the image of God, and the human body's own powers of recovery once again are made possible by God.

It has to be 'both and', when it comes to God. We must stress the importance that the God of order upholds the Universe with regularities. These regularities allow us to do science, to learn about the Universe, to marvel at the wonders of creation and they also allow us to grow in the moral sense. What would our growth be like if I pushed someone over a cliff only for God to overrule the consequences every time?

At the other extreme some have so stressed creation that God has been given no freedom at all within that creation for particular acts. Miracles are defined exclusively as 'the wonders of nature' such as the birth of a child. God is unable to do anything apart from sit back and watch. If God is moment by moment sustainer of the physical laws, then science could be seen as simply describing his normal mode of working. But God must be ultimately free to work in unusual ways.

If we see miracles in the context of a personal creator and redeemer God we should expect both his sustaining and his particular actions. Indeed we should expect a tension at times. The Bible reflects in this a tension of what we might call law and grace.

In an earlier book, I attempted to develop a personal analogy to try and express this tension.[92] Imagine parents bringing up their child. If the child is to grow up responsibly then he or she needs to know various agreed norms or rules. If the parents are continually changing their minds, the child will find it difficult to grow in understanding or responsibility. However, it would be a poor childhood if there were not special treats, times when the normal rules were superseded by special acts of love. There will be times when bedtime is normally 9pm but the highlights of the West Ham soccer game are on later and as a special treat (or not, depending on how you view West Ham United!) the child can stay up. The development of the child requires a tension between law and what the Bible would call grace, that is extravagant generosity.

If the order in the Universe is a reflection of God's faithfulness in creation, then miracles could be seen as special acts of grace when God supersedes his normal ways of working. If God did too many miracles then the world would become totally unpredictable, if he did no miracles at all it would be extremely boring! This view does not answer all the questions. In particular one may ask if God does work in this way why does he not do it more often to relieve suffering and destroy evil? But it may be that this more personal analogy for miracles is helpful in emphasising the tension or even mystery in God maintaining an ordered Universe while working in unusual ways for specific purposes.

Second, the God of the Bible both ensures our freedom and is sovereign Lord. Quite how he does this is a whole bookcase of differing volumes in a good Christian library! That God is sovereign Lord reminds us that whatever the circumstances God is working his purposes out. The concept of God's rule over all things makes it consistent both to marvel at the regularities of nature and the irregularities of the miracles. He is not a slot machine that we can use by putting enough prayers of faith in at the top, pulling the handle of the name of Jesus and expecting ready made miracles to drop out of the bottom!

That our freedom is real reminds us that we have responsibility in knowledge and in moral behaviour. We have the freedom to accept or reject the evidence that God has given of his existence and nature. We have the freedom to mess up this creation and to inflict suffering on our fellow human beings. In such a view miracles can never be proof but only pointers to a better way.

What is the place of miracles today?

In this chapter, we have reviewed some of the objections to miracles. We have seen that a simplistic but popular use of science to discredit miracles does not hold up any longer. We have seen some of the complexity of the biblical material and have left some questions unanswered. For the scientist who should be controlled by humility before the facts, this should not be a great problem. To acknowledge one's present limitation to make sense of a complex problem should be the spur to think more about these things.

However, this is not just an academic exercise. The

Christian believer or leader will be faced with questions about the miraculous almost day by day. As we read the Bible, should we expect the stories of the New Testament to happen today? Should we pray for the friend who has fallen ill? How can we with integrity affirm both science and the miraculous?

I suggest we need to remember constantly two things.

1 The sovereignty of God

At one time in Paris, there were reports of healings at the tomb of François de Paris. This caused such a sensation that the cemetery was closed by royal decree in order to stop any public disorder. By the cemetery, a local wit put up a notice which read, *By order of the King, God is forbidden to perform miracles in this place.*

We need to be very careful about prescribing what God can or cannot do. There is today a divergence within the Christian church concerning miracles. Some evangelicals argue that miracles are not for today. They suggest that miracles were needed during the special time of Jesus and the apostles, to authenticate their message. Once the Bible was formed, there was no such need and therefore claims of modern miracles are either mistaken or frauds. Some support their case by referring to 1 Cor 13:8–10:

> 'But where there are prophecies, they will cease; where there are tongues they will be stilled; where there is knowledge, it will pass away. For we know in part and we prophesy in part, but when perfection comes, the imperfect disappears.'

The argument is that now we have the Bible ('the perfect') there is no need for signs such as tongues or prophecy.

Now it is true that in the Bible miracles do seem to come in batches at particular points where they are needed such as the deliverance from Egypt, the earthly life of Jesus and the growth of the early church. However, that is not the whole story. There are 'isolated miracles' throughout the Bible, for example the miracles of Elijah and Elisha (1 Kings 18, 2 Kings

5:1–15). In addition, what is surely referred to by 'the perfect' is that time when we see God 'face to face' (1 Cor 13:12), that is heaven. To write off the many miracles which have happened throughout the history of the church in many different cultures is a very dangerous, if not blasphemous thing. Of course there will be occasions when the claims of miracles are mistaken. There will be too occasions of fraud. But we need to respect that God is sovereign in his will.

This perhaps also helps in the question of healing. Some seem to think that the miraculous is always 'on tap' to be claimed by faith. God has his own will, which is often at the time very difficult to understand. It may be that in the context of his sovereign will God does not produce miracles that we expect. Our role is to pray and ask his will to be done.

An insurance company once wrote to clergy publicising new policies. Part of the policy was the claim to insure churches against acts of God! Churches need to be places open to the will of God, expecting but not demanding miracles.

2 God is glorified in the non miraculous as well as the miraculous

Canon David Bubbers once wrote,

> 'We can read the New Testament with an eye almost solely for the miraculous and if we do it won't be long before we get restive with the seeming ordinariness of much of our church life and begin to believe that the power of the Holy Spirit is only authentic where there is noise and drama and excitement and most of all miracle. But this is not the whole picture by any means. The New Testament lays equal emphasis on righteousness, doing our duty, keeping our word, bearing and forbearing in all of our relationships. And need we doubt that many of those early Christians spent most of their lives doing just that – but no less in the power of the Spirit.'[93]

We have tried to argue that all events are God's events, whether they be the wonders of the Universe disclosed to us by science, the unusual unexplained events or the fact that God can use the regularities of the world for his purposes. For after all, what is the central core of the Christian revelation? It is a death on a cross, where the physical and biological laws of death proceeded. In the words of the singer Amy Grant, 'God's most awesome work is done through the frailty of his son'.

Miracles are only a part of Christianity. Paul wrote, 'Jews demand miraculous signs and Greeks look for wisdom, but we preach Christ crucified, a stumbling block to Jews and foolishness to Gentiles, but to those whom God has called, both Jews and Greeks, Christ the power of God and the wisdom of God' (1 Cor 1:22–24).

7

Can You Be a Scientist and a Christian?

(Rob Frost)

Scientists are explorers. They are seekers after truth. It is little wonder, therefore, that many of them face up to life's ultimate questions. History demonstrates that some of the world's leading scientists have undertaken the experiment of faith in Christ, and found that indeed you can be a scientist and a Christian.

Finding faith

Yesterday my son introduced me to the dynamic experience of 'virtual reality'! I was strapped into a small vehicle in a darkened room and exposed to the most horrifying ride of my life!

In this cinematic show entitled 'Desert Duel' I had the sensation of riding through the desert on the bumper of a heavy truck. This strange visual experience pushed up my blood pressure to danger-level because every twist and turn in the road was synchronised with my highly mobile bucket seat. When the truck dived over a cliff I felt I was about to be catapulted through the air . . . and when we hit the ground, I thought I'd done myself a serious back injury! The man at the door suggested we 'Go again' for half price; but I firmly refused! I stood in the corridor, my legs shaking, and suggesting to my son that I could really use a strong cup of tea!

If 'virtual reality' is something which tricks us into imagining that fantasy is real, 'ultimate reality' is a discovery that beyond our transient experiences of life there lies something much more real. Christians claim that when we move beyond the periphery of the transient and the finite we begin to sense something of the Eternal and the Infinite. Ultimately, we believe that God is the 'ultimate' reality.

Some scholars have noted that this sense of 'ultimate reality' has proved helpful to Christians in setting a context for their scientific research. Reviewing the work of Christians who are scientists, Olaf Pedersen, of the History of Science Department at Aarhus in Denmark noted this powerful sense of 'otherness',

> 'This insight must be a moving force behind a personal, spiritual, and moral reorientation, in so far as the mind responds to a call from something which it recognises as being outside it, and at the same time of absorbing interest.'[94]

Even if a scientist is not a Christian, it is quite possible that his work will raise questions about 'ultimate reality' for which there are no 'scientific' answers. Very often a scientist can find himself straying from questions which are purely scientific into areas that are much more theological and philosophical. Michael Poole wrote:

> 'As soon as scientists begin to ask why there is a Universe to study, or why nature operates in a regular, uniform way, or whether or not there is a mind behind the laws they observe, they are looking for different types of explanations from scientific ones.'[95]

Of course, a scientist can undertake the most radical and innovative kinds of research without once uttering a prayer or a Bible text! But even though he may not claim to be a Christian, he may well have to admit that he is wrestling with questions which are traditionally thought of as 'theological'.

Charles Darwin, for instance, went to Cambridge to prepare for ministry in the Church of England. Later on, however, his journey on HMS *Beagle* on a five year voyage around the world (1831–6) focused his attention on natural history. He challenged the fixed nature of species in *The Origin of Species* in 1843, and this led him into a major controversy with other scientists and the general public.

Darwin struggled with Christianity, especially after the death of his daughter, Annie, yet later in his life he was still able to say: 'In my most extreme fluctuations I have never been an atheist in the sense of denying the existence of a God.'

Beyond the boundaries

The mystery at the boundaries of human experience has parallels in the world of the arts. Artists also claim an ability to dream impossible dreams and to see possibilities which no one else can see. The Christian artist and the Christian research scientist work at the edge of human imagination and in this way they look beyond the accepted norms of their day in the hope of glimpsing something infinitely greater.

The Christian faith recognises God's presence in the world and sees him as the sustaining force behind all created things. Christians who are working at the frontiers of human knowledge sometimes feel that they are actually in touch with what God is doing. Albert Einstein, though not Christian, also had an awareness of the 'theistic'. He wrote of:

'A rapturous amazement at the harmony of natural law, which reveals an intelligence of such superiority that, compared with it, all systematic thinking and acting of human beings is an utterly insignificant reflection.'

Scientists, then, are explorers, and the sense of 'otherness' which scientific research can evoke within them can sometimes lead them on to search for the meaning of life itself. Many scientists throughout history have wrestled with these ultimate questions, and some have found that Christianity provides the right context for answering them.

It's strange going back to places which you knew many

years before. Yesterday, I was surfing in the huge Atlantic breakers of Perranporth in North Cornwall. The experience was exhilarating, and it brought back memories of how it felt to surf on a thin white piece of board on the same beach when I was a teenager over thirty years ago!

More memories were unlocked when I walked alone beside the roaring surf as the big red sun set over the horizon. I could clearly picture myself standing at the same spot one night, looking up at a starlit sky, and wondering 'Who made it all?'

That, along with many other formative experiences, led me to a belief in God the Creator, but it was only the starting point for my journey towards Christianity. It was the mysterious figure of Jesus which clinched things for me.

In one of my long debates with a church youth leader, I remember disputing the validity of Christ's miracles. Eventually the leader looked me in the eye and said, 'There's only one miracle to believe, Rob, the miracle that he came! If you accept that, you'll have no problems with the rest!'

Christ at the centre

Jesus is not just an idea and his existence as a real and historical figure is something supported by external historical sources. The historian Sir James Frazer said that 'the doubts which have been cast on the historical reality of Jesus are, in my judgement, unworthy of serious attention.'

The Jewish historian Flavius Josephus wrote: 'And there arose about this time a man called Jesus – a wise man if indeed he should be called a man.'

The New Testament writers were in no doubt as to his reality, either, for Saint Peter declared, 'We have not depended on made-up legends in making known to you the mighty coming of our Lord Jesus Christ. With our own eyes we saw his greatness. We were there when he was given honour and glory by the Father!'

Professor F F Bruce, in a masterly review of all the evidence available, wrote in *New Testament Documents: Are they*

Reliable? that the 'earliest propagators of Christianity welcomed the fullest examination of the credentials of their message. The events which they proclaimed were, as Paul said to King Agrippa, not done in a corner, and were well able to bear all the light that could be thrown on them.'[96]

The effect of this one life on two thousand years of world history is also convincing evidence as to his reality. J N Geldenhuys observed that 'the whole course of world history during the last nineteen hundred years is inexplicable apart from the historical fact that Jesus Christ lived, died and rose again.'

The concept of the Incarnation is at the heart of Christian faith. The mystery and wonder of it cannot be proved, but it does make sense! Some years ago I was at Cliff College in Derbyshire when astronaut James Irwin spoke of his disastrous career as a test pilot. He had suffered multiple injuries in an air crash, but it was this 'near death experience' which finally led him to faith in Christ.

At the conclusion of his talk he presented to the college a large colour picture of himself standing on the moon, and inscribed the words *It is more significant that God walked on Earth than that man walked on the Moon.*

When, in my late teens, I came to the gospels with a fresh hunger to understand Jesus and to weigh the disturbing claims that he made, I found myself fascinated by the stories which I'd taken for granted as a child. As I re-read them with greater maturity and understanding the reality of his love and care seemed to shine from every page. It was the quality of his compassion, care and servanthood which rang true, and which gave me an insight into God's character and being. At last, I came to faith in him myself.

The heart of love

From his early days as a refugee in Egypt, to a hostile reception in his home town of Nazareth, he knew rejection. He was treated cruelly by the religious establishment of his day and knew injustice and a false trial in Jerusalem. Even those who were closest to him betrayed and deserted him. Yet there was no hint of bitterness in him.

He called children to him; reached out to untouchables; and cared for the despised and broken people of his generation. He mixed with the outcasts, the losers, the drop-outs and the poor and helped them to wholeness.

Hear his words of forgiveness and see his promises of healing fulfilled. Glimpse him breaking the bread and pouring the wine, and promising a New Kingdom. Watch him hanging on a cross at Calvary and declaring 'Father, forgive them.' His love shines from every word and deed of his ministry and makes him attractive and different. It's little wonder, therefore, that when Swiss theologian Karl Barth was asked to define his most profound concept in Christianity, he replied, 'Jesus loves me, this I know, for the Bible tells me so!'

Cliff Richard wrote, 'If this love is true – then it has to be the most radical, urgent and relevant piece of good news ever to be delivered. Personally, I am as convinced of it as I am about anything.'

Why did he love? Richard Bube, Professor of Materials Science and Electrical Engineering, at Stanford University, California, reviewed the evidence and concluded:

> 'God has taken the attributes of his being – his love, his mercy, his holiness, his justice, his power – and has translated them into a form that men can understand, believe and respond to ... The climax of God's revelation of himself is the person of Jesus Christ. In him the ultimate and the unconditional are wed to the transient and the conditioned in such a way that a human being can respond with his or her own personality.'[97]

This life of Perfect Love gives us a clear pointer as to how we should live, and how human society was designed to function. Christ's ministry was not just about loving deeds, however, for he made important claims which need to be addressed and tested.

Considering the claims

He was sinless, yet he could forgive sin, and he warned that he would be the judge of the world. He said that he could give eternal life, could answer prayer, and had authority over all things. He told others that he was the truth, the object of faith and that he was worthy of worship.

He equated himself with God and claimed that to know him was to know God, to see him was to see God, to believe in him was to believe in God, to receive him was to receive God, to hate him was to hate God and to honour him was to honour God! It's little wonder, therefore, that Oxford don C S Lewis declared, 'Either this man was the Son of God – or he was a madman or something worse,'

In the Gifford Lectures, entitled *Religion in an Age of Science*, Ian G Barbour saw Jesus as the distinctive revelation of God:

'We can accept all that science tells us about our evolutionary history and biochemical functioning. We can at the same time acknowledge the unique features of human, mental, cultural and religious life. Beyond that, we can without inconsistency portray a special role for the person of Christ within this historical framework.'[98]

His incarnation and resurrection marked him out as different from every other human being. The brilliant French General Napoleon said, 'I know men, and there is no term of comparison between Jesus and any other man who ever lived.'

The philosopher Rousseau concluded that 'If the life and death of Socrates are those of a philosopher – the life and death of Jesus Christ are those of a God.' Jesus was unique and different. Christians believe that he is truly God, yet truly man.

If, as Christians claim, Jesus is God incarnate – come among us to demonstrate perfect life and perfect love, then any search for life's ultimate meaning should at least include an examination of this one intriguing life.

As we have seen in the previous chapter the evidence for his resurrection is very strong indeed. The descriptions of his resurrection have been sifted and tried by many scientists, lawyers and historians over the years; and as a result many have become convinced by the evidence available. In reviewing the life of Christ, Arthur Peacocke, former Fellow of Biochemistry at St Peter's College and now an Anglican priest wrote:

> 'The fact is that in Jesus the Christ his Jewish followers encountered, especially in the light of his resurrection, a dimension of that divine transcendence which, as devout monotheists, they attributed to God alone. But they also encountered him as a complete human being and so experienced an intensity of God's immanence in the world different from anything else in their experience or tradition.'[99]

Christians consider that Jesus, therefore, was far more than a great teacher, leader or philanthropist. He is God Incarnate. His life was a life of perfect love, his teaching was a message of perfect compassion, and his work in the lives of countless people today is a work of perfect grace.

Beginning with the Bible

After I had come to faith in Christ I began to want to understand the Bible. I was a member of a fairly crazy youth group, and our debates about the Bible were, in hindsight, rather immature. We must have had a very patient leader! It was this exposure to the Bible that helped to ground me as a Christian, and which gave a shape and structure to my faith. I began to realise that the Bible was not just a book of doctrine, but an unfolding record of God's dealings with mankind.

I discovered that the Bible was not a story or a thesis, but a mix of many different styles of writing, including proverbs, poetry, parables, epics, prophecy, history, prayers, songs, personal letters, paradoxes and allegories. I found that this diverse collection of literary documents serves many different purposes. Parables are not historical data, historical descriptions may not have a spiritual meaning, and sermons may not have a descriptive purpose. Some passages are historical, some symbolic and others are both. Above all, it's not a scientific textbook!

Maybe those who study scientific journals for a living find the Bible less approachable than others! Howard Van Till, a Professor of Physics and Astronomy, stated:

> 'Twentieth century culture seems to me particularly inept at understanding and using figurative or symbolic literature. We are so accustomed to straightforward, matter-of-fact descriptive prose that we expect nearly all writing to be of that form . . . Scientific writing has made an illegitimate claim of superiority over artistic literature.'

The Bible is neither straightforward nor dull! It was written over a period spanning 1,500 years by more than forty different authors from different walks of life, and representing over forty generations. David was a king, Moses was a national leader, Amos was a herdsman, and Luke a physician. Parts of it were written in Asia, Africa and Europe and in Hebrew, Aramaic and Greek. It was written from many different historical backgrounds, personal experiences and national perspectives.

We must come to the Bible with a different set of expectations than when we open any other book. Richard H Bube observed:

> 'Just as science cannot be done without faith in its possibility, so the revelation of God cannot be understood and expounded in theology without commitment to His existence and self revelation. In both cases the wisdom of the commitment in faith can be tested at least to some extent by examining its consequences and actions based upon it.'[100]

What is the Bible, therefore? Christians believe that its main theme is the destiny of the Universe as told through one story and one plan of redemption. Its main purpose is to answer man's deepest needs and his most burning questions. Christians approach the Bible with faith, and test its relevance and authenticity in their everyday lives.

Perhaps, more than most readers, scientists will want to know if the material being examined is reliable and trustworthy. In this regard, the science of archaeology has made an immense contribution to the Bible's authenticity.

Can archaeologists help?

William F Albright notes that during the twentieth century there has been a rapid increase in the number of serious archaeological expeditions from different countries and a phenomenal improvement of archaeological method. This new methodology has greatly helped with the analysis of superimposed layers of occupation, and the classification and relative dating of the objects found. The rapid growth of new techniques derived from natural sciences has helped, most especially through the use of radiocarbon for dating. The decipherment and interpretation of the flood of new inscriptions and texts in many scripts and languages which were unknown until recent decades has also proved revolutionary. Albright concludes that: 'Archaeological and inscriptional data have established the historicity of innumerable passages and statements of the Old Testament.'

Archaeology has confirmed the culture and custom of Abraham's day, it has brought to light the great Hittite Empire previously unknown to historians, and proven the accuracy of Luke's writings at every point which is verifiable. Sir William Ramsay set out to uncover contradictions between the Biblical records and actual archaeological findings; but after years of extensive archaeological research in Asia Minor and Greece he was forced to conclude:

'I take the view that Luke's history is unsurpassed in regard to his trustworthiness ... You may press the words of Luke in a degree beyond any other historian's and they stand the keenest scrutiny and the hardest treatment.'[101]

Archaeology does not prove the Bible to be the word of God, but it can confirm the basic historicity of a narrative. It is supported by archaeological evidence again and again, in both the general and the specific, such as the names of places and persons turning up at the right places and in the right periods.

The Bible scholar and the scientist have much in common in that they are both engaged in a search for truth. When Julius Bewer described Biblical criticism he could have been describing a scientific experiment!

'A truly scientific criticism never stops. No question is ever closed for it. When new facts appear or a new way of under-standing the facts is shown, the critic is ready to re-examine, to modify or overthrow his theory, if it does not account for all the facts in the most satisfactory way. For he is interested in the truth of his theory, and indifferent to the label, old or new; orthodox or heterodox; conservative, liberal or radical, that others may place upon it.'[102]

First and foremost, however, we turn to the Bible if we want a Christian understanding of God. Whilst an open mind and a desire for the truth may lead us to explore textual criticism, we need to take care in case it obscures the Bible's central message.

The scientist who is a Christian must seek the truth using the best resources of Biblical scholarship, but he must also approach the Bible with a hunger to understand what God is really saying through it. He needs to read the lines rather than between them!

A leap of faith?

The journey of faith takes people down different routes, but often a mysterious sense of 'otherness', the magnetism of Jesus, and the relevance of the Bible are important markers along the way.

Jonathan Edwards is a contemporary example. This 18:29 gold medalist triple-jumper, and one of Britain's few world champions, graduated with a good degree in science from Durham. The only job he could get was at the Royal Victoria Infirmary in cytogenetics. Working on chromosomes, analysing bone marrow specimens from cancer patients, and reflecting on the fact that forty-six chromosomes contain all of the information about every human body convinced him that God was responsible for it all!

'To believe that from total chance came humanity, flowers, birds, sky . . . obviously I came from the point of view that God created the earth and everything in it.'

He gives glory to God for his record breaking wins, and testifies 'God has been with me through the ups and the downs, and has brought me to this tremendous place where I can present the gospel to people. Because there will be judgement, and for those who do not know Christ, everlasting punishment awaits.'[103]

The wonders of creation, the life of Jesus, and the authority of the Bible bear witness to the truth of Christianity. History is full of human witnesses – like Jonathan Edwards – who claim that they have tested Christianity, and found it not wanting!

Science researchers who have come to faith discover that they approach their work with a new sense that God has created things to some design and order. This enables them to believe that the laws of nature are understandable and that the cosmos has a purpose.

Many Christians sense this divine 'purpose' in their research. Science history records the stories of many Christians who had a deep awareness of God's power, and whose lives illustrate that you can be a Christian and a scientist!

Buridan

I don't pretend to understand the laws of motion, but I certainly experienced them first-hand one day on the spectacular rollercoaster at Alton Towers! The sense of inertia as we left the ground station and the strange sensation of powerlessness as we sped along upside down remain with me to this day!

We can see the laws of motion in action first-hand by playing with the executive toys which grace many desks up and down the land. Lift the end ball and drop it against the rest and they will all happily swing to and fro in irritating regularity for some considerable time.

Much of the early work on motion was done by a Christian philosopher called Buridan in the fourteenth century. His thinking was daring and revolutionary because his laws of motion directly opposed the theories of Aristotle, theories which had held sway for over fifteen hundred years! Throughout this fifteen hundred year period the progress of scientific research had been hampered by Aristotle's thesis of motion, and no one throughout the educated world dared suggest that Aristotle might have got it wrong!

Buridan's work on the laws of motion led him to suggest that at the point of creation God set all the particles of the cosmos in motion, a kind of motion that would enable them to continue according to the impetus given to them. He attributed the origin of motion to his Creator.

Although Buridan's ideas about motion might sound reasonable to us today, they were very revolutionary in the fourteenth century! Buridan's laws led to the science of motion and, some historians claim, to the early development of science itself.

It was Buridan's faith which led him to call into question Aristotle's propositions, and his understanding of God that enabled him to identify the laws of motion. Buridan's sense of God's activity as the 'first cause' of motion was central to his thinking. Again and again in history there are stories of scientists like Buridan whose strongly held Christian views led them to question the theories of the scientific establishment.

John Major

Another famous researcher was the Christian scholar called John Major (the scientist – not the politician!). It is difficult for us to imagine what it must have been like for Major to work as a scientist in late medieval times with such limited scientific knowledge and so little understanding of the size of space.

John Major based his thinking on the possibility of there being a void space, and of God being powerful enough to create or destroy matter anywhere even beyond the known stars. He argued that God could even create an infinite number of worlds beyond our own.

His thinking reached far beyond that of his contemporaries, and expressed his personal desire to discover even more of God's greatness. Major was able to glimpse a greater Universe because he worshipped a God of infinity and eternity.

Major's faith in a God of unlimited greatness led him to take on the religious establishment of his day and to look beyond the long-held scientific theories of his contemporaries. His faith in a God of infinite greatness inspired him to question the established theories of his time and so to pioneer new work on the size of the Universe.

Copernicus

Copernicus was another Christian who 'dreamed a bigger dream'. His controversial writings *On the Revolutions of the Celestial Spheres* written in stages between 1512 and 1542 and published in 1543 described some of the most significant scientific discoveries in history.

Copernicus could see elements of God's purpose in the order and design of the Universe, but he was also keenly aware of God's supreme power at work there. These aspects of his faith enabled him to conceive of theories which contradicted what his contemporaries were saying. As he studied the movement of the stars and planets he came to recognise that the Sun was the centre of things, and not the Earth.

Later, Copernicus's work led him to the disturbing conclusion that the dimensions of the Universe must be at least two thousand times larger than had previously been thought! He went on to suggest the possibility of an infinite Universe. He saw the immeasurable distance of the fixed stars as consistent with the greatness of 'this divine work of the great and noble Creator.'

Time and again Copernicus indicated in his work that he was motivated by his belief in a great God. Historians are satisfied that he was not just writing to placate theological critics but out of a real and committed faith.

Scientists like Copernicus have approached their work with a sense of God's supreme greatness and power. This attitude has helped them to lift their eyes above the accepted norms of scientific theory and to seek the supernatural activity of God beyond the limits of human understanding.

Paraclesus

Paraclesus is well known to those who work in chemistry or medicine. He was a lay preacher who worked among miners and peasants in Austria and Switzerland in the first half of the sixteenth century. Paraclesus based his revolutionary ideas on the teaching of Jesus that 'the sick have need of a physician' (Mark 2:17). He taught that Jesus would only have said this if doctors were a part of God's plan to heal the sick.

The Parable of the Good Samaritan struck a chord with Paraclesus, and he saw his medical work as a direct response to this story and the commission of Jesus to 'love your neighbour'. He took this commission personally and used every means possible to cure people. He recognised that medical work must flow from a love for those in need, and not as a means of getting money!

Paraclesus believed that every illness would eventually be cured, a belief which, in his time and culture, was a revolutionary concept. Diseases like epilepsy seemed beyond cure and new health problems like the plague were breaking out in many places. Some felt that they would never be cured.

Paraclesus' simple faith in God led him to research the causes of illness. He discovered that diseases like the plague came from outside the body by infection and were not simply imbalances of the body's 'humours'. He began to investigate the possibility that infection affected particular organs, and searched for chemicals which might fight these influences.

Modern medicine still builds on the foundations of Paraclesus' work. His principles on infection resulted in a more analytical approach to the structure and function of the body and an interventive kind of medicine using chemicals targeted at specific organs.

Christians who are working as scientists, like Paraclesus, often have a rich sense that they are discovering the features of a created world. They see the world's design and order as an expression of God's purposes.

Kepler

One of the greatest scientists to emerge from the Reformation was the Lutheran Johannes Kepler. His three laws, which are the basis of modern astronomy, came out of his desire to describe the orbits of the planets in purely mathematical terms. Historians tell us that Kepler's faith was the motivating impulse for his research. Kepler once prayed: *I give you thanks, Creator and God, that you have given me this joy in thy creation, and I rejoice in the works of your hands. See I have now completed the work to which I was called. In it I have used all the talents you have lent to my spirit. I have revealed the majesty of your works to those who will read my words, in so far as my narrow understanding can comprehend their infinite richness.*

This prayer illustrates the way in which science and faith can co-exist together in one person's life. The Christian researcher does not have a schizophrenic personality, with faith and work in exclusive watertight compartments! Rather, he recognises the activity of God both in his own life, and in the research he is conducting. The research itself can become a potent expression of his faith in action, driven on by a commitment to Christ and a vision to serve humankind.

Occasionally moments of new understanding within a research project can feel like moments of divine revelation. Scientists have often felt that God is active in the work they are doing, and that, in the doing of it, they are about something sacred.

The physicist Bragg wrote:

'When one has sought long for the clue to a secret of nature, and is rewarded by grasping some part of the answer, it comes as a blinding flash of revelation: it comes as something new, more simple and at the same time more aesthetically satisfying than anything one could have created in one's own mind. The conviction is of something real, and not something imagined.'

Robert Boyle

Boyle's work is known by all students of physics and chemistry. Using a pump he performed a variety of experiments to conclude that the apparent power of the vacuum was due to the difference in air pressure between the evacuated cavity and the surrounding atmosphere. Boyle calculated that the volume of a gas decreased in proportion to the mechanical pressure exerted on it, a principle commonly known as 'Boyle's Law'. In *The Usefulness of Experimental Natural Philosophy* (1663) he wrote:

'. . . methinks we may, without absurdity, conceive that God . . . did divide . . . the matter, which he had provided, into an innumerable multitude of very variously figured corpuscles . . . that by the assistance of his ordinary preserving concourse, the phenomena which he intended should appear in the Universe must as orderly follow . . .'

Kepler, then, could see in his research 'the work of God's hands' and Boyle recognised that God allowed his sustaining power to reveal 'the phenomena which he intended should appear.' They both saw the world as something given by God, and this sense of 'givenness' was at the core of their scientific activity.

Dr Arthur Peacocke is the Director of the Ian Ramsey Centre at St Cross College, Oxford. He reflected on the way that scientists encounter God when they recognise his activity in the Universe when he wrote:

> 'The affirmation of the existence and transcendence of God is, then, a response to the sheer givenness of it all. The need for such a response is, if anything, enhanced by the scientifically perceived subtlety and rationality of the observed Universe. The response involves the recognition of God as Creator, of God as giving being to all – that is, of God as the ground of all being, as being itself; and of the world as having a derived and dependent being.'[104]

Isaac Newton

Isaac Newton (1642–1727) was one of the best-known scientists to advocate Christianity. The second half of seventeenth century science history was dominated by Newton's discoveries in the areas of absolute space and the operation of principles like gravity to mediate between different bodies.

His faith was always central to his work. In a letter to a friend he wrote 'the Rotations of the Planets could not be derived from Gravity, but required a divine Arm to impress them.' He actually wrote *Principia Mathematica* with an eye to sharing his faith with others, and his aim was that he might persuade them 'for the belief of a Deity.' In the 1713 edition of the same work he added the following note:

> 'He is not eternity and infinity, but eternal and infinite; he is not duration or space, but he endures and is present. He endures forever, and is everywhere present; and by existing always and everywhere, he constitutes duration and space ... he is omnipresent not virtually only, but also substantially ...'

Newton saw God as the 'first cause' of all things, in whose love and grace we find a sense of wholeness which nothing else can bring. His work was intimately connected with his Christian experience, and there was no division between his faith and his research. He wrote: 'There is but one God the

Father of whom are all things and we in him and one Lord Jesus Christ by whom are all things and we by him.'

Faraday, Joule and Maxwell

Faraday, Joule and Maxwell were three important nineteenth-century scientists who all professed Christianity. Michael Faraday's principal contribution to scientific discovery was his work on electromagnetic induction – a means of generating an electric current using magnets. When he observed the pattern of magnetic filings suspended over a magnet, Faraday developed the concept of magnetic lines of force, and in 1845 he introduced the term 'magnetic field' to describe the structure of the pattern.

His own evangelical faith gave him a structure for his research. His starting point was that nature was the product of a rational mind and that its laws are comprehensible, that it has a unity and that it runs autonomously.

James Prescott Joule (1818–89) was the son of a wealthy Salford Brewer. His research in Manchester led him to identify the First Law of Thermodynamics, and in the three papers advocating this principle (1843, 1845, and 1847) he made repeated reference to God, arguing that energy cannot be annihilated because 'that power belongs to the Creator alone!'

James Clerk Maxwell (1831–79) is remembered as the founder of the electromagnetic theory of light and as a pioneer in thermodynamics. He wrote: 'I have looked into most philosophical systems and I have seen that none will work without a God.'

He repudiated materialism and was suspicious of a completely determinist view of physics. He said 'Christians whose minds are scientific are bound to study science that their view of the glory of God may be as extensive as their being is capable of.'

This famous mathematician and physicist once prayed: *Teach us to study the works of Thy hands that we may subdue the earth to our use, and strengthen our reason for Thy service.*

It is interesting that all three of these nineteenth century scientists found that their research strengthened their faith rather than undermined it, and that each of them praised God for his greatness.

William Bragg

The English physicist William Henry Bragg (1862–1942) was born into a farming family in the Northwest of England. He studied mathematics at Trinity College Cambridge and devoted a lot of his thinking to the relationship between Christianity and science. During a lecture at the Royal Institution in London in 1919 he said

> 'From religion comes a man's purpose; from science, his power to achieve it. Sometimes people ask if religion and science are opposed to each other. They are: in the sense that the thumb and fingers of my hand are opposed to one another. It is an opposition by means of which anything can be grasped.'

After University he taught mathematics and physics at the University of Adelaide in Australia for over twenty years. At the age of forty-one, inspired by the new advances in X rays and radioactivity he began a series of experiments which won him international acclaim and professorships at Leeds and later in London.

As a physicist Bragg emphasised the importance of experiments over theories, of which he was always very suspicious. After years of experiment in order to prove the 'corpuscular' nature of X-rays he rejected the theory when his experiments demonstrated the wave nature of X-rays.

Bragg won the Nobel Physics prize in 1915 for his analysis of crystal structure by means of X-rays. The year before his death he delivered a lecture on 'Science and Faith' in which he emphasised the experimental basis of scientific and religious knowledge.

> 'Science is experimental, moving forward step by step, making trial and learning through success and failure. Is not

this also the way of religion, and especially of the Christian religion? The writings of those who preach the religion have from the very beginning insisted that it is to be proved by experience. If a man is drawn towards honour and courage and endurance, justice, mercy, and charity, let him follow the way of Christ and find out for himself that it leads him where he could go.'

Science and faith are not incompatible. It is the interaction of the two which makes for truth and wisdom. Professor A N Whitehead wrote: 'Science . . . religion . . . On the one hand there is the law of gravitation, and on the other the contemplation of the beauty of holiness. What one side sees, the other misses; and vice-versa.'

Science and faith

These examples from the history of science could be multiplied many times over, not to mention the many present day scientists who hold a Christian faith.

However, the big questions about meaning, the existence of God and life after death are not exclusive to scientists. People all over the world wrestle with the same issues as they face up to life's disappointments, heartaches and mysteries. Sometimes this questioning leads them to God. Christians believe that Jesus Christ is the answer to these questions, and that they have found in him a sense of destiny, meaning and value which nothing else can bring.

Each Christian's testimony is different, yet there are often common echoes in them all. Kris Akabusi, for instance, the Olympic gold medal winner, found Christ as he struggled to find something more satisfying than materialism. 'No sooner than I'd got something, there was something else I wanted. I began to think that there had to be another meaning to life.'

The answer came during the Commonwealth Games in 1986 when he found a Bible in his hotel room and began to read about Jesus Christ.

'When I realised these things about him, I knew that I had a decision to make. I started investigating to find out if what he said was true. One night, a few months later, I simply prayed, *Lord, if you are there, and I really don't know if you are, you'd better come and say Hi to Kris!*'

This simple prayer led him to a life-transforming experience which changed his personal goals, his relationship with his wife, and his perspective on the future. It was a moment of 'seeing'.

Many prominent scientists have reached similar periods of dissatisfaction with life, and in facing life's big questions have discovered that Christ is the answer.

Many scientists can testify to a life enriched by Christ, and even of a sense of his presence in the demanding work of research. A panel of sixty scientists and technologists involved in the Methodist Report *Shaping Tomorrow* stated:

'We have outlined our intellectual grounds for belief in God primarily to support our contention that, in order to accept the Christian gospel, it is not necessary to make any 'leap of faith' in contradiction to our intellectual reasoning.'

Faith is not something which goes contrary to our intellectual processes, for the use of reason is an important part of the struggle for faith. Reason, however, cannot take us the whole way. When someone becomes a Christian he is not abandoning his intellect, quite the reverse. Our reason and intellect leads us to an appreciation of our need for God, and to a respect for the authenticity of the Christian message.

When reason has taken us as far as possible along the road to Christianity, however, there comes a time for us to 'test out' the experiment of faith. It is faith which enables us to prove Christianity for ourselves. It is time to discover, like Bragg, that the experiment proves the theory and not vice-versa!

Seeing for yourself

John Houghton, the Chief Executive of the Meteorological Office from 1983–1991, has written about the scientific experience of 'seeing' in his book, *The Search for God*. Many of us can remember moments when 'the penny dropped' or we got a flash of inspiration. He makes special reference to the work of eminent mathematicians who sometimes have experiences of solutions coming to them 'in an instant'. He concludes:

'It is not surprising that 'seeing' is a term that is often used about religious belief. Contrary to the popular phrase, faith is not blind; it is something we acquire when we 'see'; we talk for instance of the eye of faith. Sometimes this insight comes in a flash, as with Paul on the Damascus Road, sometimes it develops much more slowly. As with scientific 'seeing', after the first sight, faith needs to be tested in a whole variety of ways.'[105]

When I was a teenager I stood beside a deep ravine and held on to the rope swing suspended above me. I looked up at the rope and wondered if it would take my weight, and at the branch on the tree above to check that it wouldn't break! I looked down at the ravine, and shivered at the thought of what would happen if I fell! But then my friends shouted 'Go for it Frosty' and I launched out into space as an act of faith. The experience was superb, and my faith was rewarded!

Over the years it has been my privilege to pray a 'prayer of faith' with people from a diverse range of backgrounds as they have leapt out beyond the security of reason to take part themselves in the great 'experiment of Christian faith'.

One weekend I struggled with questions put to me by a group of medical students at a University in Wales. They gave me a particularly hard time, and I began to count the hours to the end of the conference! To my amazement, however, as the final service drew to a close I saw three of them move forward to pray 'the prayer of faith'.

I made this experiment of faith when I knelt alone one night in a wood in Warwickshire, and it is an act of faith which has proved its worth in my life ever since. Millions of Christians from all kinds of backgrounds and walks of life have experienced this kind of 'seeing' faith for themselves . . . and many of them are scientists!

Nigel Cutland is a Professor of Mathematics at the University of Hull. When he was twenty years old he accepted an invitation from fellow students to join them for coffee and discussion about the meaning of life. They leant him a book called *Mere Christianity* by C S Lewis, whose arguments made sense to him as a mathematician.

Although he was convinced intellectually it took him over eighteen months to make a personal commitment to God and to move from 'understanding' to 'seeing'. He recognised that knowing about God was not enough and that he needed to take a 'step of faith'. This experience of 'seeing' led him to a very different view of life.

> 'To have a relationship with the God of the Universe has given me a real sense of purpose and security about knowing who I am and where I am going. That sense of purpose pervades my whole life. As a mathematician, knowing that what I am doing is within the framework and design of the Creator makes it very worthwhile. It's also a big help to me to know that it is God who has given us minds and has made a world which is to be investigated and discovered. Another great joy for me as a Christian is the sense of belonging to a family, people who accept and love me. It shows me that God's love is real.'[106]

When any experiment is complete, and the results have been checked and cross-checked, there comes the time to reflect on what the exercise has proved, and how we see things differently in the light of the new discovery.

As I have talked to scientists about their work and faith in the preparation of this material, it has struck me again and again how integrated their science and their faith has become. As stated earlier, the faith really does enrich the science, and the science the faith! We should not really be surprised, for, as John Polkinghorne observed, Jesus Christ is the connection of all things!

'He is the source of connection, the one whose creative act holds in one the world-views of science, aesthetics, ethics and religion, as expressions of his reason, joy, will and presence. This interlocking character of the world of creation finds its fullest expression in the concept of sacrament, an outward and visible sign of an inward and spiritual grace, a wonderful fusion of the concerns of science and theology.'[107]

After the seeking is over and the arguments are finished, the time comes for a decision. There is no other way. No one can be argued into the Kingdom of God. All that I can do is to share the good news of a God who is alive, of a Saviour who loves us, and of a Spirit who is active in the mysterious processes of the Universe.

When the message is delivered, I have done my job. The time has come to test the evidence, to apply reason to the big questions of reality, and to launch out and trust Jesus Christ as Lord and Saviour. Perhaps the time has come for you, the reader, to test the experiment of faith for yourself and to discover that you can, indeed, be a scientist and a Christian!

Further Reading

We hope that after reading this book you may want to follow up in general or by focusing in on more specific questions:

Popular introductions to the relationship of science and Christianity:

R Forster & P Marston, *Christianity, Evidence and Truth* (Crowborough: Monarch, 1995)

J N Hawthorne, *Windows on Science and Faith* (Leicester: IVP, 1986)

R Holder, *Nothing but Atoms and Molecules* (Tunbridge Wells: Monarch, 1993)

J T Houghton, *The Search for God: Can Science Help?* (Oxford: Lion, 1995)

J C Polkinghorne, *Quarks, Chaos and Christianity* (London: Triangle, 1994)

M Poole, *A Guide to Science and Belief* (Oxford: Lion, 1994)

D Wilkinson, *God, the Big Bang and Stephen Hawking* (Tunbridge Wells: Monarch, 1993)

J Wright, *Designer Universe* (Tunbridge Wells: Monarch, 1994)

More academic treatments of the relationship of science and Christianity:

I G Barbour, *Religion in an Age of Science* (London: SCM, 1990)

R Hooykaas, *Religion and the Rise of Modern Science* (Edinburgh: Scottish Academic Press, 1972)

D M MacKay, *The Open Mind* (Leicester: IVP, 1988)

A R Peacocke, *Creation and the World of Science* (Oxford: OUP, 1979)

A R Peacocke, *Theology for a Scientific Age* (London: SCM, 1990)

J C Polkinghorne, *One World* (London: SPCK, 1986)

J C Polkinghorne, *Science and Christian Belief* (London: SPCK, 1994)

C A Russell, *Cross-Currents: Interactions between Science and Faith* (Leicester: IVP, 1985)

Scientists writing about the origin and structure of the Universe:

J D Barrow, *The World Within the World* (Oxford: Clarendon, 1988)

J D Barrow, *Theories of Everything* (Oxford: Clarendon Press, 1991)

J D Barrow and F J Tipler, *The Anthropic Cosmological Principle*, (Oxford: OUP, 1986)

P Davies, *God and the New Physics* (Harmondsworth: Pelican, 1983)

P Davies, *The Mind of God* (New York: Simon and Schuster, 1992)

S W Hawking, *A Brief History of Time* (London: Bantam, 1988)

S W Hawking, *A Brief History of Time – A Reader's Companion* (London: Bantam, 1992)

S W Hawking, *Black Holes and Baby Universes* (London: Bantam, 1993)

J V Narlikar, *The Primeaval Universe* (Oxford: OUP, 1988)

R Penrose, *The Emperor's New Mind* (Oxford: OUP, 1989)

Books on the Genesis text:

H Blocher, *In the Beginning* (Leicester: IVP, 1984)

D Burke (ed.), *Creation and Evolution* (Leicester: IVP, 1985)

D Kidner, *Genesis* (Leicester: IVP, 1967)

E Lucas, *Genesis Today* (London: Scripture Union, 1989)

Books arguing for a six day creation:

K Ham, *The Lie Evolution* (El Cajon: Creation Life Publishers, 1990)

D R Humphreys, *Starlight and Time* (Colorado Springs: Creation Life Publishers, 1995)

H M Morris, *Scientific Creationism* (Edinburgh: Christian World Publishers, 1974)

J C Whitcomb and H M Morris, *The Genesis Flood* (Grand Rapids: Baker, 1961)

Scientists arguing that science 'does away with God':

P Atkins, *Creation, Revisited* (Oxford: W H Freeman, 1993)

R Dawkins, *The Blind Watchmaker* (Harmondsworth: Penguin, 1988)

R Dawkins, *River out of Eden* (London: Weidenfeld and Nicholson, 1995)

Christian responses to questions of science ethics:

D Cook, *The Moral Maze* (London: SPCK, 1983)

R Elsdon, *Greenhouse Theology* (Tunbridge Wells: Monarch, 1992)

L Osborn, *Guardians of Creation* (Leicester: Apollos, 1993)

C A Russell, *The Earth, Humanity and God* (London: UCL Press, 1994)

J Stott, *Issues Facing Christians Today* (Basingstoke: Marshalls, 1984)

On miracles:

C Brown, *That You May Believe* (Grand Rapids: Eerdmans, 1985)

C S Lewis, *Miracles: a Preliminary Study* (London: Fontana Books, 1967)

J C Polkinghorne, *Science and Providence* (London, SPCK, 1989)

M Poole, *Miracles: Science, the Bible and Experience* (London: Scripture Union, 1982)

On the historicity of the New Testament:

C Blomberg, *The Historical Reliability of the Gospels* (Leicester: IVP, 1987)

F F Bruce, *The New Testament Documents: Are They Reliable?* (Leicester: IVP, 1960)

References

Chapter One

1 R Moore, J Buckley & N Newman, *Behold the Front Page!* (Edinburgh: Mainstream Publishing Company, 1993)
2 R Dawkins, *River out of Eden* (London: Weidenfeld and Nicholson, 1995)

Chapter Two

3 S W Hawking, *A Brief History of Time* (London: Bantam, 1988) p. 175
4 P Davies, *The Guardian*, May 4th 1995
5 J C Polkinghorne, *The Guardian*, May 3rd 1995
6 Quoted in 'Genetic Revolution', *M.D. Magazine* August 1979, p. 77
7 J N Hawthorne, *Windows on Science and Faith* (Leicester: IVP, 1986) p. 57
8 M Doughty, The *Tablet*, October 1988
9 F Hoyle & C Wickramasinghe, *Evolution From Space* (London: J M Dent, 1981)
10 F Crick, *Life Itself: Its origin and nature* (London: MacDonald, 1981) pp. 15–16
11 W Paley, *Natural Theology* (1802) in *The Works of William Paley*, ed. R Lyman (London, 1825) pp. 8–9
12 A Einstein, Quoted in *Science News*, March 31st 1979, p. 213
13 J Balchin, *What Christians Believe*. A Lion Manual (Oxford: Lion, 1990) p. 62

14 L Barnett, Quoted in *The Universe and Dr Einstein* (New York: Morrow, 1957) p. 95

15 E Jantsch., *The Self Organising Universe* (Oxford: Pergamon Press, 1980) p. 80

16 N Gerrard, *The Observer*, June 11th, 1995

17 C P Michael & M C Norrisey, *Prayer and Temperament* (New York: The Open Door Inc., 1991) p. 112

18 M Muggeridge, '25 Propositions on a 75th Birthday', *The New York Times*, April 24th 1978

19 M Morse, *Transformed by the Light* (London: Piatkus, 1992)

20 See for example D M Mackay, *The Open Mind* (Leicester: IVP, 1988)

21 M Ruse, *Darwinism Defended* (Reading, Mass: Addison Wesley, 1982) p. 108

22 J B S Haldane, *Possible Worlds* (London: Chatto and Windus, 1930) p. 62

23 J C Polkinghorne, *One World* (London: SPCK, 1986) p. 97

24 S W Hawking (ed.), *A Brief History of Time – A Reader's Companion* (London: Bantam Press, 1992) p. 140

Chapter Three

25 J Nehru, *Proceedings of the National Institute of Science of India* 27A (196) 564. Quoted in M Perutz, *Is Science Necessary? Essays on Science and Scientists*, (Oxford: OUP, 1991)

26 Quoted in A Toffler, *Future Shock* (New York: Random House, 1970) p. 87

27 L Wolpert, 'Religious thinking does not produce knowledge,' *The Times*, April 10th 1993

28 R Dawkins, 'Writer donates £1m to strike blow for theology,' *The Independent* March 18th 1993

29 B Russell, *The Problems of Philosophy* (New York: OUP, 1912) p. 17

30 M Perutz, *The Times Higher Educational Supplement*, November 25th 1994

31 B Russell, *Religion and Science* (Oxford: OUP, 1972) p. 243

32 R Dawkins, *The Independent*, December 23rd 1991

33 B Appleyard, *Understanding the Present: science and the soul of modern man* (London: Picador, 1992) p. 249

34 E Schrodinger, *Nature and the Greeks* (Cambridge: CUP, 1954)

35 P Medawar, *The Limits of Science* (New York: Harper and Row, 1984) p. 66

36 G Zukav, *The Dancing Wu Li Masters* (London: Flamingo, 1989) p. 331

37 J H Brooke, *Science and Religion – Some Historical Perspectives* (Cambridge: CUP, 1991)

38 R Hooykaas, 'The Christian Approach to Teaching Science,' *Science and Christian Belief* **6**, no 2, 113 (1994)

39 M B Foster, 'The Christian Doctrine of Creation and the Rise of Modern Natural Science', *Mind*, **43**, 1934, 446; **44**, 1935, 439; **45**, 1936, 1. See also R Hooykaas, *Religion and the Rise of Modern Science*, (Edinburgh: Scottish Academic Press, 1972), C A Russell, *Cross-Currents: Interactions between Science and Faith*, (Leicester:IVP, 1985); S L Jaki, *The Saviour of Science* (Edinburgh: Scottish Academic Press, 1990)

40 T Wakeford & M Walters (ed), *Science for the Earth: Can Science Make the World a Better Place?* (John Wiley, 1995) p. 75

41 Mackay, op. cit., (20) p. 102

42 J Calvin, *Institutes*, III, 2, n. 15

43 R Dawkins, 'A scientist's case against God', *The Independent*, April 20th 1992

44 J Polkinghorne, *One World* (London: SPCK, 1986)

45 P Parker, *To Know as We are Known: A Spirituality of Education* (New York: Harper and Row, 1983)

46 M Poole, *A Guide to Science and Belief* (Oxford: Lion, 1990) p. 40

Chapter Four

47 J Stott, *Issues Facing Christians Today* (Basingstoke: Marshalls, 1984) p. 280

48 R Chadwick, *Ethics, Reproduction and Genetic Control* (London: Routledge, 1987) p. 95

49 Stott, op. cit. (47), p. 30

50 A van den Beukel, *God and the Scientists* (London: SCM, 1990) p. 68

51 C Merchant, *Physics World*, June 1995

52 J Mahoney, *Bioethics and Belief* (London: Sheed and Ward, 1984) p. 96

53 van den Beukel, op. cit. (50)

54 H Blamires, *The Christian Mind* (London: SPCK, 1963) p. 70

55 D Cook, *The Moral Maze* (London: SPCK, 1983) p. 45

56 Stott, op. cit. (47), p. 35

57 J E Haught, *The Cosmic Adventure* (Paulist Press, 1984)

58 Stott, op. cit. (47), p. 43

59 John Polkinghorne, *Science and Providence* (London: SPCK, 1989) p. 86

60 Sir Nevill Mott (ed.), *Can Scientists Believe?* (London: James, 1991) p. 106

61 Cook, op. cit. (55), p. 56

62 *The Times*, August 12th 1995

63 Mott, op. cit. (60), p. 32

64 Haught, op. cit. (57), p. 61

65 J C Sawhill, *Science* 206 (4416): 281 (1979)

66 R Sperry, *Science and Moral Priority* (Oxford: Blackwell, 1983) p. 106

67 Haught, op. cit. (57), p. 167

68 J T Houghton, *The Search for God: Can Science Help?* (Oxford: Lion, 1995) p. 214

69 A Peacocke, *Theology for a Scientific Age* (London: SCM, 1990) p. 343

70 C Kaiser, *Creation and the History of Science* (Grand Rapids: Eerdmans, 1991) p. 89

Chapter Five

71 *The Big Bang*, dir. J Toback, Kanter-Toback Productions, 1989
72 See for example E Lucas, *Genesis Today* (London: Scripture Union, 1989)
73 I owe this illustration to Dr Roy Clements
74 R F R Gardner quoted by D English, *Preaching*, Abingdon, USA, 1995
75 H C G Moule, *Colossian Studies* (London: Hodder and Stoughton, 1898) pp. 81–82
76 R Forster & P Marston, *Christianity, Evidence and Truth* (Crowborough: Monarch, 1995) p. 25
77 Quoted in O Gingerich, 'Let there be light: Modern cosmology and biblical creation', Paper presented at the joint meeting of Research Scientists Christian Fellowship and the American Scientific Affiliation, Oxford, (1985)
78 Quoted in M Poole, op. cit. (46), p. 109
79 Lucas, op. cit. (72), p. 151
80 D Wilkinson, *God, the Big Bang and Stephen Hawking* (Tunbridge Wells: Monarch, 1993) and *In the Beginning God*, (London: Home Mission Division of the Methodist Church, 1990)
81 J D Barrow, ' Universe began in no time at all,' *The Observer*, May 7th 1993
82 C A Coulson, *Science and Religion: A Changing Relationship* (Cambridge: CUP, 1955) p. 7
83 S W Hawking, *Black Holes and Baby Universes* (London: Bantam, 1993) p. 90
84 Quoted in M Rowan-Robinson, 'Flying in the Face of God,' *The Guardian*, October 28th 1993
85 J Kepler: Life and Letters, *Kepler to an unidentified nobleman*, October 1623, p. 114–15

86   R Boyd, *Science and Christian Belief* Vol. **6**, No 2 (1994): p. 143

Chapter Six

87   J Wimber with K Springer, *Power Evangelism* (London: Hodder and Stoughton, 1985) p. 77
88   C S Lewis, *Miracles: a preliminary study* (London: Fontana Books, 1967) p. 102
89   H G Alexander (ed.), *The Leibniz-Clarke Correspondence* (Manchester: Manchester University Press, 1956) p. 18
90   J P Crutchfield et al, 'Chaos,' *Scientific American* 255 (1986): p. 38
91   Houghton, op. cit. (68), p. 81
92   Wilkinson, op. cit. (80)
93   D Bubbers, *The British Weekly* October 24th 1985

Chapter Seven

94   O Pederson, *Physics, Philosophy and Theology. A Common Quest for Understanding* (Notre Dame: University of Notre Dame Press, 1988) p. 65
95   Poole, op. cit. (46), p. 72
96   F F Bruce, *The New Testament Documents Are They Reliable?* (Leicester: IVP, 1960) p. 22
97   Mott, op. cit. (60), p. 117
98   I G Barbour, *Religion in an Age of Science* (London: SCM, 1990) p. 213
99   Peacocke, op. cit. (69), p. 301
100 Mott, op. cit. (60), p. 118
101 W M Ramsey, *Luke The Physician* (London: Hodder, 1908) pp. 77
102 Julius A Bewer, *Journal of Biblical Literature* Vol. **47** (1929–30): pp. 305–379
103 The Valerie Grove Interview, *The Times*, August 11th 1995

104 Arthur Peacocke, *The Challenge of Science to Religion* (The Templeton Lectures, RSA, 1993)
105 Houghton, op. cit. (68), p. 216
106 N Cutland, 'There is Hope,' *Jesus Magazine* 1995
107 Polkinghorne, op. cit. (23), p. 97

Index